Leroy Calder

D0983907

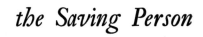

the Saving Person

the Saving Person

by ANGUS DUN

HARPER & BROTHERS, PUBLISHERS

New York

Library of Congress catalog card number: 56-12065

to REINHOLD NIEBUHR, *dear friend*

CONTENTS

Foreword

This little book would not have been written save for an invitation from the faculty of the Yale Divinity School to deliver the Lyman Beecher Lectures in 1956. That invitation came as a command. Its acceptance constrained me to write against all the resistances within and without. Left free to choose any topic relevant to the work of the ministry, I decided to strike as nearly as I could at the center. The heart of the minister's calling is to open to men the salvation offered in Christ. The Christian religion in all its unfolding variety is the way of salvation through Christ. Putting books aside, I tried to write simply, with a fairly minimal use of traditional terms, in the hope of freshening the well-worn theme

for myself and others. Unconsciously, to begin with,
I found myself returning again and again to a word
much used by my admired friend, Paul Tillich, "the
ultimate," though he must not be held responsible if I
have been untrue to his wisdom. Through what I have
written there runs the conviction that the immediacies
of life and the ultimates of life cannot be pulled apart.
The Saving Person, the Ultimate Person, entered into
and accepted the immediacies of life. The Kingdom
which He bids us seek invades the world of everyday. To be reconciled to God is to be reconciled to
life itself in all its concreteness. The eternal is the
realm of resurrection in which the actualities of this
life are lifted up and redeemed.

To write is to be afraid and to stand under judgment. For what is written is written and cannot be
changed. One wishes it were more worthy of the
theme and of the Lenten Season in which it is pub-
lished.

ANGUS DUN

the Strange Word, Salvation   I

the Immediacies and the Ultimates of Life

There is an ancient phrase in the service of ordination in the Book of Common Prayer in which the ministry is described as "so weighty a work pertaining to the salvation of man." At once this phrase sets us wrestling with the deepest and the most central questions of our calling. What have we to offer men? What is at the heart of our task?

As the answer to these questions, salvation is one of the most uncompromising words that comes to us out of our inheritance, more particularly salvation through Christ. An ancient creed, widely treasured among us, speaks of One "who for us men and for our salvation came down from heaven."

Salvation through Christ is what we have to offer

to men. The heart of our task is in some manner to bring this salvation within reach of men and help them to appropriate it. But what is this mystery named salvation and how is it offered or given through that other mystery named Christ?

There are many approaches possible in struggling toward an answer to these hard questions. We could plunge directly into the meaning of some of the classical utterances of Christian faith on this subject. We could add another little secondhand essay to the volumes of the history of this theme. Perhaps it is wiser not to plunge into the center directly, but start further off. Certainly most of the people with whom we deal do not feel at home in the center of this theme. Their thoughts and concerns seem far removed from salvation. If we begin at a tangent we shall be starting where they start. And since we are not so unlike them perhaps we shall be starting where we truly find ourselves.

We know well that men—we ourselves, people around us, men everywhere—meet with evils and goods on many levels; we struggle for deliverance from these evils and for the possession of these goods. If salvation is taken in so broad a sense as to mean simply deliverance from the evils of life and the achievement of its goods, then all men are concerned.

We can remind ourselves sketchily of the various levels and areas in which men meet with evils from which they seek deliverance and goods they strive to possess.

Man has a bodily life, an animal life. He is a hungry creature. He is bound to the earth and to things earthly by his needs. Without food and water and air he suffers and sickens and dies. He is hurt by too much cold or too much heat. He needs shelter from the sun and from the winter. When too hot he joys in coolness. When too cold he delights in warmth. He lusts and seeks the ecstasy of sexual release. Man is easily bruised and broken or poisoned. Hostile organisms enter his body and he is racked with fever. The chemistry of his body goes wrong and he withers away. He has an age span. Given the most favorable conditions he nevertheless ages and dies. Even at this level there is in him a will-to-live, a struggle for existence of which death is the final—and not too significant—defeat.

If man were simply an animal his problems and his satisfactions at this level would be far simpler than they are. But to be human is also to be possessed of a mind and an imagination. The consequence is that all of man's wants and deprivations, even at this most elementary level, are open-ended. He does not simply hunger and seek food and eat. He savors and experiments and dreams of more tasty food. He remembers and imagines and explores in all the areas of bodily satisfaction, and is never satisfied. His wants are endless, and his deprivations.

In all of this struggle for satisfaction nature is alike his friend and his enemy. She provides and withholds. Out of this elementary human situation issues one of the most characteristic marks of man, that he is a worker. Food does not fall into his lap. He has to go and get it. Fish do not jump out of the water. They are more appetizing when cooked. They do not remain edible unless frozen or smoked. When the cold wind blows nature offers little cover. Man has to fashion a covering for himself.

So work is an inescapable part of our human situation. If anyone does not work because of privilege or sloth or sickness or lack of opportunity he can live only because others work for him. From this fact spring all the burden and the blessing of human labor, from the simplest processes of food-getting and shelter-building to the most elaborate technology applied to the mastery of nature. And because the wants are endless the work is endless.

Moving to another level, man is a social creature. He can exist and grow in human stature only in com-

munity. He needs his fellows even for his animal
life. Man seeks woman and woman seeks man. And
straightway when man confronts his fellows deeper
realities emerge. Communication begins. Companionship is born. Face answers to face. Language follows
quickly. Meanings leap from the interior of one life
to the interior of the other life, always imperfectly.
All the rich variety of man's responses to, and relatedness with, his fellows is found, love and hate, fear
and friendship, co-operation and conflict. Every aspect
of his bodily life is taken up into his life with his
fellows and gains new dimensions. Food is fought
over and also shared, and in being shared life is shared.
Sexual union and the birth of children bring with them
a deep sense of mutual belonging between man and
woman and between parents and children. Men both
gather under one roof and destroy one another's
shelter. Men are knit together in sickness and in
health. They can hurt or slay one another. Death
takes on new meaning. It is not only the defeat of the
will to live; it can eliminate an enemy or take away
one greatly needed or greatly loved. Everywhere and
always man finds it impossible to live without his
fellows and hard to live with them.

As social creature man lives in groups. However
he expresses it he knows the meaning of belonging.

This is his family or tribe or village or people. He identifies himself with the ever-expanding communities of relationship and of labor of which he is a member and the community claims him as one of its own. The fortunes of the community are his own, its prosperity or dearth or catastrophe, its victories or defeats, its enmities toward other communities. There are communal memories and communal hopes.

Within man's life in community there emerges inescapably the order of relationships we call politics, the problems of order and law and rule. Whether it be in a community as small and simple as a family or a tribe, or a community as large and complex as a people or a nation, life is intolerable without order. And order is not to be had without rule or some centralization of power. Politics in broadest terms has to do with the ordering of the forces which struggle together in human community. These forces move in individual lives and in the groups within the community. They draw men together and set them against one another in ever-changing patterns. They represent every level of motivation by which men are moved—hunger, desire for land, the search for raw materials, the struggle for minerals, oil, trade; and along with these economic ends the desire for security in personal property; the will-to-power; pride of race or nation; and more ideal motives such as will for independence or love of freedom or even passion for justice. Wherever community is found there are centers of rule whose function is to maintain order, if it be only the elders in a family or if it be chieftain or governor or king. And the order they maintain is always partly tolerable and partly intolerable. So community always exists in tension.

It is plainly impossible to deal with any one level or area of man's life and being without spilling over into others because man is of a piece. Even the satisfactions and deprivations of his animal life are profoundly interwoven with thought and imagination. His life in community would be impossible without the capacity to see himself as related to his fellows and to share with them meanings and hopes and fears. His intelligence first emerges as the servant of his most elementary wants and expands in its range with the endless multiplication of his interests. It rarely escapes wholly from this servitude. Man finds patterns of relatedness in nature which he eventually conceives of as causality. He observes connections between water and crops, between warmth and decay, between the length of a lever and the weight it will lift. He explores, experiments, invents to satisfy his wants. But his mind does not remain purely instrumental. It breaks free and seeks its own satisfactions in its search for rationality, coherence, order, meaning in the manifold of experience. So he makes for himself world pictures, always with the indispensable help of his imagination, and is uneasy when confronted by the unintelligible.

But man's response to nature and his fellows is not simply that of a creature of elemental desire and of a would-be knower. He is an aesthetic being. There is that within him which in many measures answers to shapes, to patterns of color and of sound, to rhythms of light and shade, of line, of words. He contemplates the changing color on distant hills and listens rapt to the sound of running water and the song of birds. And, more wonderful, under the impulsion of this delight he re-creates nature in the forms of art. He draws pictures on the walls of his caves. He gives pleasing shape to his shelter and adds color to his clothing. He invents drum and lute and violin and organ. He composes music. He molds his utensils beyond all the demands of utility. He gives rhythm to his words. He reworks his personal and communal memories and imaginings into dramatic forms that communicate not only the truth of his situation as he sees it but the felt meaning of it, its tragedy or comedy

or glory or darkness. In his artistic creations he holds
a mirror up to life. He may, on the other hand, find
in them an escape from the harsh realities and demands
of his existence.

There is still another level of relationships which
must have a crowning place in any sketch of man.
When men confront one another in personal meeting
or in community there is not only a struggle or a
flowing together of hunger with hunger, of desire
with desire; there is not only some meeting of minds
and some aesthetic attraction or repulsion. Men make
claims one on another. "Thou shalt not take my
food." "Thou shalt not take my wife." They pass
judgments on one another. They admire and condemn one another's manner of acting and even the
make-up of the person from whom the action issues.
They learn to isolate and identify what they admire
and what they condemn. Quite universally they admire
courage, the capacity to go forward in the face of
hurts and dangers, and loyalty to the group of which
a man is a member. Equally they condemn willful
cruelty or treachery to the group. They formulate
laws to express the claims which all make upon each
and sayings to embody their judgments. In all this
there is much self-interest and much will-to-control.
But confusedly there also appears within it that high

and distinctive reality we call man's moral being.

Not only do men make claims on one another, they know what it is to stand under claims. They may even condemn themselves and know the strange uneasiness of not being able to accept what they have done or what they are. Along with the endless goods that beckon to desire and the endless evils that threaten pain or defeat, there are goods that bring a distinctive constraint. In man an "I ought" is rarely, if ever, wholly lacking, however obscured or distorted or impoverished in content. This whole aspect of life can develop only in social relationships. It is so largely embodied in the pressures and claims of social custom and social demand that the conclusion lies ready at hand that it is nothing more than a social manifestation. But conscience once born can outrun all custom and all law. In creative individuals it formulates for itself claims of justice and of mercy and of personal excellence under which society itself stands condemned. And human societies pay an uneasy tribute of approval to their moral spokesmen.

We can probably agree that most men most of their waking hours are living at these various levels in which they meet with evils from which they seek deliverance and goods they strive to possess. They are eating and drinking and working at their jobs.

Periodically they respond to the urgencies of sex. They are building or improving their dwellings. They are conversing with their fellows, complaining about their governors, worrying about the threat to their group by some other group, rejoicing in a victory, trying to understand better how nature works or why their fellows behave as they do, delighting for a time in some beauty, and wondering marginally, for the most part, what they ought to do.

Does all this provide clues for the meaning of that ancient word "salvation"? It can be observed that when a man or a community is confronted with an issue of life and death the word "save" is likely to be spoken. A child is "saved" from drowning. A man is "saved" from death by penicillin. When a community is confronted by such a measure of internal disorder or of economic chaos as to threaten its very being as a community, the leader who restores order may earn the title of "saviour of his country." It has been claimed that the Marshall Plan "saved" Western Europe. These situations present themselves as ultimate. Everything is at stake. But the issues that have this character are not confined to those in which the bodily life of an individual or the material being of a community is radically threatened. There is another death than the death of the body. A job may be the "saving" of a man, not only or not chiefly because it provides him with a means of existence, but because it restores meaning and shape to his existence. When a man is the victim of alcoholism, Alcoholics Anonymous may be his salvation because it restores his disintegrating manhood to human stature. A homeless or neglected child, unloved and fearful and resentful, may be saved by adoption into a healthy family. It is not only that bodily life is secured but that the opportunity for total human fulfillment is given. There are situations that present us, or seem to as we confront them, with issues of ultimate loss or ultimate gain.

Let us follow this clue. At all the levels and in all the areas of his life man presses toward a limit and finally confronts an ultimate which presents questions for which he greatly needs an answer.

Man quickly identifies conditions near at hand which determine his fortunes, whether food is given or withheld, whether children are born, health or sickness, the well-being of his community. But his inquiring imagination presses past the conditions near at hand toward an ultimate ground, toward determiners of destiny or a Determiner of Destiny, toward an ultimate Giver or Withholder. How does it happen that this is given and that withheld? Why is anything given?

There is an empty place in man's outreaching mind and imagination waiting to be filled. And it will be filled with some image or idea, fate, nature, spirits, Spirit, willy-nilly. How this empty place is filled makes a profound difference. For man with all of the conflict and diversity within him has a sense of wholeness and struggles toward wholeness. And any human community with all of its inner conflict and diversity has some wholeness or ceases to be. Man has some underlying attitude or disposition toward the total manifold of life. And this attitude is deeply conditioned by the effective image of what ultimately confronts him. Is "It" friendly or hostile or just neutral or indifferent? Have I, as an individual, any meaning for "It"? Have we together any meaning for "It"?

Man the picturemaker presses inescapably toward some total picture of his situation. Man the storyteller and the poet presses toward some total rendering of the drama of his existence. By some picture of life he will live. Is humankind set in a vast realm of chance like a rolling ball in a gambling machine? If they feel that the answer is affirmative, men will live nervously or recklessly, irresponsibly watching for the "breaks" and cursing their ill luck, hoping that they may fall into the right hole and ring a big bell and produce the jackpot. Or is life pictured as the struggle of the

strong to consume the weak and does man rejoice
when he is strong or resent his weakness? Is man a
waif found unaccountably on the doorstep of Mother
Nature, who is beautiful but dumb? Is life an unac-
countable chance to snatch some fleeting pleasures,
high or low according to taste, but ending in meaningless darkness? Are the high things that stir in man, the
desire for inner cleanness of motive, the respect of
common men for honesty or unselfishness, the trou-
blings of conscience and the aspirations of the seers,
but crude animal urges disguised to look pretty? Are
they passing fashions in human preference? Or are
they rooted in the hidden depths of being?

By some overruling picture of life man will live or
his life will be distracted and torn apart by shifting ad-
justments to conflicting pictures that fade out and are
replaced by others, like the pictures on a moving
film. He will fill the vacant place in his outreaching
mind with some image or images. And the answers he
finds to his ultimate questions will flow back into all
the levels and areas of his life. They will enter into
as elementary a thing as his eating, determining according to the hold they have whether his food is
simply snatched, or received in gratitude and gladly
shared. They can greatly shape his work, determining

whether it be a curse or a heady competition for top place or even a calling.

Man is like a child in a family. He can tolerate much deprivation, much sickness, even much pain, if only he be securely at home, sure of belonging, confident of being loved. But if these central assurances are lacking then food and shelter and toys in abundance can leave him empty and insecure in the center of his life. So it is with man in his world.

Man presses out toward a limit as he looks into his setting and seeks to apprehend what finally confronts him and determines his destiny. Likewise man the desirer, man the empty creature seeking to be filled, man who can live only by taking the stuff of his world up into himself, presses toward a limit. His satisfactions are commonly so partial and so passing. His unfolding hungers and needs lead him on and on. He lives by bread but not by bread alone. He lives by working, by companionship, by loving and being loved, by knowing, by absorbing beauty and creating a little of it, by answering to claims that come to him. The question can come to him, Is there some best good, some pearl of great price, which he might gain and not hunger again. Or the question may come in reverse. Is there some deepest evil which to escape would bring final release? Is that deepest evil to hunger and not to be filled? Is it pain? It is aloneness? Is it death? Is it guilt, the self-reproach of knowing that one has not fulfilled the claims which life offers? Is there some ultimate escape from these evils or some ultimate victory over them?

Man the social being, man in community, man the political animal, man confronted with the claims he meets in community, is likewise led step by step toward ultimate issues and questions. His experience with his fellows of knowing and being known is good but partial. He longs to know fully and to be fully known, and dreads it too. Is there some perfect companionship, some perfect knower, who knowing yet accepts? The communities within which men find themselves never remain completely self-enclosed. That other community which speaks differently, dresses differently, acts differently, looks differently, penetrates into our community or threatens it. They are different yet so much alike. Could it be that those which differ are our kind too? What is the ultimate community?

The order men achieve in community is always imperfect order. There is strife and recurrently open conflict. It can threaten existence or make existence intolerable with bitterness and fear. Men struggle for the perfect order which will bring peace and justice. In periods of high enthusiasm they even believe that they have found it—the democratic order or the communist order. If only this order could cover the earth then we would have arrived. Men dream, at least, of a perfect king or order.

Man in community meets with claims, commands, rules, and laws coming to him from many directions. They come from parents to children, from elders, from institutions, from rulers. "Don't bounce your ball by the china closet." "Keep yourself clean." "Obey your father." "Be brave." "Support your community." "Treat every man as a person." "Fight for your country." "Thou shalt not kill." "Drive slowly." "Fulfill your contracts." "Pay your taxes."

All of these and endlessly more like them are designed to guard something good. They serve their purpose even though that purpose is often clouded and distorted by man's perversity in seeking to impose his self-will on others. But they become confusing and burdensome. They sometimes conflict with one another. Certainly they conflict with man's desires, with what he takes to be his own good, and with his will to be his own master. Are there some ultimate laws that could give simplicity and wholeness to the claims under which man stands? Is there any ultimate reconciliation between law and desire or law and freedom? Few persons explicitly ask these questions but generally they are wrestling confusedly with the issues involved in them.

Every human society finds itself driven to sustain its most crucial laws by the dark ways of compulsive power, by the coercions of fines and imprisonments and death. But no human society is sound and secure if these penalties are the main supports for the overruling claims which the community makes upon its members. There must be majesty in the law if there is to be spontaneous obedience. So the ultimate question becomes, "Whence comes that Majesty?"

The lives of individual men and the life of a human community are greatly shaped and energized by what we can call objects of devotion. There is a release which comes to individuals when they are caught up in the enthusiastic service of something beyond themselves to which they can give themselves with a high measure of completeness. This experience gives unity to individuals and binds men together over against the pull of their cross-purposes. Men need objects of devotion and they find them. If they do not find one they will find another—a gang, a family, a college, a nation, a hero, science, art, world order. The most powerful forces in history are communities of devotion, and the most divisive. Here again men press toward a limit. What is the object of ultimate devotion? Is there any such ultimate object?

So another stage is reached in this search for the meaning of that word "salvation." To be concerned with so "weighty a work" is to be focused as steadily as may be on the ultimate questions and issues of human life. It is to be doing business out at the limits. That is a high calling, presumptuous, always somewhat suspect. The minister's work is to confront men with the final questions, to awaken their deepest hungers and to help them find the final answers, to escape the ultimate evils and gain the ultimate goods. In sober realism he must recognize that while there is that in the human situation that presses men toward the limits, they are largely absorbed in things nearer at hand. If the ultimate questions have a fascination, they are also disturbing and demanding. Men are drawn to them and withdraw from them to find refuge in the familiar immediacies. Men demand that they be met where they live and be served on the level of the recognized goods and evils of common life. They demand that ordinary sociability be provided, immediate hopes encouraged, established loyalties and devotions strengthened. The ultimate issues most commonly come alive when men "come to the end of their rope" or touch what seems to them ultimate joy; in the face of death or radical illness, when the foundations of community seem to be crumbling, at marriage or birth or in times of great deliverance.

Thus far the theme of salvation has been approached from the manward side, in terms of man's wants and needs and questionings. But the human situation would be very different from what it is if no answers had been given and no goods presented to provide substance and definition to man's wants. Even the most elemental hungers are greatly modified and enlarged by what is given. On the level of food men may hunger for bread alone until offered beans or beef or broccoli or beer. A political order may maintain itself for centuries until disturbed at its roots by the presentation of an alternative order. How much more is this the case at the level of man's ultimate needs and questionings.

Here it is necessary to take a great leap.

A look back into history or out on the contemporary human scene discloses many ways of salvation being offered to men and men responding to them. Some of these ways bear the name of religion. Some of them would repudiate that name and appear rather as political and economic movements. All of them have this in common that they offer men deliverance from what they present as the ultimate evils and participation in what they present as the ultimate goods. They differ widely in their interpretation of what ultimately confronts men and where they find the focus of man's ultimate problems. It is impossible to review them all as they have emerged in history or played their part in the world of our own time. But samplings are significant.

Among the ways of salvation offered, two radically contrasting types may be identified. There are the ways which say "No" to all the interests and strivings of man's everyday life and summon him to seek a good which lies quite outside of them. And there are the ways which seize upon some good or bundle of goods which emerges within the common stuff of this-world existence and exalt it into the ultimate position to claim allegiance and to offer the fulfillment of man's best hopes.

An ancient way of salvation sees men burdened with pain and sorrow and frustration and purposelessness, rooted in the obsession of desire for that which can never satisfy. Selfhood and suffering are inseparable. By a radical surrender, by giving up the passionate will to live, to propagate, to possess, to gain power, man can find an ultimate peace.

Closely akin to this way are the recurrent movements in the history of thought and striving which find in death the ultimate evil. Everything in the world is given over to passingness, to change and decay. But over against the passing things of time there are timeless, abiding goods, even a timeless One untouched by all the passing. The way of salvation is to escape as well as one may from the prison house of the bodily and all the ties that bind to the dying world and to float off into eternity. And of that final floating off man can gain, if he will follow the way of detachment, ecstatic anticipations even in the midst of time.

How utterly different is the way of salvation, more implicit than explicit, in many segments of our American way of life. We are caught up in the dynamic movement of a great community ever crossing new frontiers in the mastery of nature, ever enriching life with new satisfactions, new sensations, new victories over disease and poverty. To be a member of this community and to share its dreams is enough to give meaning to life. Or is it?

At any rate there are more confident movements in our world, less confused apparently by misgivings as to their finality. There is the one with which we are almost tiresomely preoccupied, communism. Fanatical men, greatly believing, promise to build by violence a paradise for the deprived multitudes of the world. Willingly the believers postpone the hitherto little known freedom-to-choose to gain freedom-from-want, and those not willing are compelled. Freedom-to-choose will come later, they say, when the basic bondage has been broken. Is this for them a service which is perfect freedom?

Alongside this movement, so inviting to many and so threatening, youthful nationalisms stir powerfully throughout Asia and Africa to counterbalance the recurrent nationalisms of the West. They release the pent-up and frustrated hungers and energies of whole communities of men. They feed on the resentments built up through centuries against alien domination, against being treated as an inferior breed. They promise a great deliverance, shared conquest over the niggardliness of nature, an abundant life, restored human stature and a standing erect among peoples of the earth as any man's equals, or even superiors.

All these movements, illustrative of the second way, have this in common that they engage men deeply in the this-world enterprise. They are often too easily dismissed as being "materialistic." But that diagnosis is too simple. It is true that they are all much concerned with the physical basis of human life, with food and shelter, with the land and the fruits of the soil, with technical mastery over nature and victories over bodily disease. But they also offer goods of larger dimensions. Even human reproduction is given larger meaning. Our children will be servants of this ongoing community of life and they will share, even if we do not, in the greater glories that lie ahead. Work is given higher meaning. We are builders together of these dams and factories and skyscrapers and nuclear reactors. A wider companionship is offered, "fellow Americans," "Comrades," fellow citizens of the "New India" or the "New China." Delight is found and pride taken in the beauty of one's own land, in the beauty fashioned by one's forefathers, in the creations of the gifted ones among us. All this is ours together. All of these movements, each with its distinctive wholeness, holds out to men a many-sided bundle of goods. So they can serve as objects of devotion releasing men in a measure from the service of themselves, giving wholeness and fulfillment to their individual lives and binding them together. If it were not so they could not so easily take on the character of a way of salvation, an answer to ultimate needs.

Man's ultimate needs and questionings are largely shapeless and undefined until they are confronted with some way of salvation. Facing two radically contrasting ways which give shape to ultimate strivings, we are committed to salvation through Christ.

A distinctive mark of salvation through Christ is that it offers a third way, we might say a middle way. It holds together the here and the beyond. It points men beyond all the goods and evils of their everyday this-world life and yet finds this beyond penetrating deeply into the stuff of common life. This third way we shall seek to explore.

the Saving Person 2

Those of us who dare to think that
we are called to "so weighty a work pertaining to the
salvation of man" stand confronting the human scene.
We find our fellows, and ourselves with them, deeply
immersed in the immediacies of life, yet pressing out
confusedly toward ultimate questions and ultimate
needs. We do not pit ourselves, emptyhanded or
emptyheaded, against these ultimate questions and
needs. There is put into our hands the record of a life,
the strange, familiar story of one who bears the human
name of Jesus. He belongs to a far-off time and a far-
off place. Yet He is spoken of mysteriously as belonging to the present, as living "above," even as
coming. And straightway it is plain that what we are
given to work with is not chiefly another picture of

the world, another total view of things to be set
against the many men have drawn, though that is
included. We are given a picture of the world or
better, a rendering of the total drama, but this record
is at the center. We are not given chiefly another set
of heavy demands or claims to be laid upon men,
though that is included. We are given the record of
a saving person. This record is reported to be good
news for men, decisively good news. All through the
story and all around the story is the testimony that in
the coming of this Person into our world something
has happened, or is happening or will happen—which
is it?—of ultimate meaning and power for men everywhere. New possibilities of life are declared to be
opened up. With the story comes an urgent pleading
invitation to men to appropriate and make their own
what has happened in the coming of this Person, that
they may be sharers in the ongoing movement of new
life originating in His coming. Whatever else may be
said, our calling is to bring the meaning and power
of this Saving Person to men by any means available,
by interpretative words, by sacramental action, by
personal witness. He came to save that which was
lost. By His stripes we are healed. He is bread of the
world. He is our peace. In Him is life.

What manner of person is this whose story is put

into our hands? To know this Person, as to know any person, is to know what He thinks, what He cares for, what He does, how He is related to His fellows, the meaning of His life for others. For some persons there is a total meaning widely shared which identifies the person. So for us Americans Washington is the Father of our Country; Lincoln is the Great Emancipator. For a still wider human community Einstein is the discoverer of relativity. The total meaning of this Person named Jesus, is gathered up in many different phrases, always including the title of The Saviour.

To know this one named Jesus whom witnesses declare to be the Saving Person we must enter into His way of looking at things, His way of dealing with the stuff of life and His total meaning for those in the whole drama of whose lives he has a decisive role. All of these are wrapped up in one bundle. What we call His teaching is part of Him and the whole action of His life illuminates His teaching.

He confronts and deals with the many levels and areas of our life. He accepts them as part of experience. He finds them good after their kind. Yet He always points beyond them. He comes eating and drinking. He bids men seek for daily bread. It is good that the hungry be fed, that the thirsty be given a cup of cold water, that the naked be clothed. It is good that a sheep be pulled out of a hole and even better that a man be pulled out of a hole. It is good that heavy burdens be lifted from men and bad that burdens too heavy to carry be loaded on them. It is good to kill a fatted calf for a returning son and even to put a ring on his finger and to have music and dancing. He knows that men have need of all these things. He is greatly concerned with those who are bruised and with the sick. He is a healer, seeking to make whole those who are broken. He appeals constantly to man's native will-to-live. While He does not marry a wife, He plainly accepts as good the desire which draws a man to a woman and a woman to a man and makes of the two one flesh. He speaks of this desire as one could only if He understood it from within. For a time He shares in the world's common labor and when He turns to another calling He works at it with a consuming sense of urgency. He finds men working in the fields, working in their households, working in the care of their sheep, and speaks well of those who work diligently, faithfully, with intelligent foresight.

Obviously all the familiar given relationships of man to man concern Him greatly. He finds good the relationships of father and son, of brother with brother, of friends, of neighbors. The breaking of relationships by enmity or alienation is evil and the restoring of relationships is something to be striven for and rejoiced in. He knows what it is to belong to a particular people and loves the city which is the center and the symbol of that common life. He accepts the need of men for government and governors. The tribute due is to be given even to an alien Caesar.

With the most ambitious adventures of the human mind He is not specifically concerned. Philosophers and scientists are not noted in the world of His experience. Yet He is a philosopher in His own way, seeking to see things whole and to help men penetrate into the depths of being. And He certainly appeals to men's intelligence and speaks often of their folly and their misreading of the facts of life.

He does not deal with art and its place in human life, though He rejoices in the bright array of the lilies of the fields and recognizes that Solomon had his glory. He is an artist, nevertheless, a gifted storyteller and One whose words are shaped into rhythms that delight the ear.

When we turn to the claims under which men stand and to the whole area of man's moral life none will deny that the One of whom we are speaking is wholly at home. There are even those who would say that this concern for morality is His specialty. He acknowledges the claims of parents on children, of masters on servants, of neighbor on neighbor, the constraints of another man's possessing on our will to possess, of another man's will-to-live on our own will-to-live. He speaks much of fair-dealing and common kindness. He would not undercut or destroy any of these claims.

So it is that this One who is for us the Saving Person is at home with, and says Yes to, all the immediate goods of our this-world life. But He always points through them and beyond them to an ultimate. Man shall live by bread but not by bread alone. Every good thing we find in life, just because it is good, threatens to take the central, overruling place in our striving. And every evil as confronted tends to present itself as the all-consuming evil. The Saving Person would deliver us from this delusion. We must not let what we shall eat or how we shall be clothed become the central anxiety of life. We may treasure the dear relationships of our family, but our family is not the ultimate family. We must be loyal to our community but give our final loyalty to the ultimate community. We give our allegiance to earthly rulers, but our final allegiance is given to an ultimate King. There is joy in a marriage feast, but He speaks of an ultimate marriage feast. There is a joy that is called blessedness.

We may hold fast to the gift of life in ourself and in others, but we dare not imagine we can gain it by clinging to it anxiously. All the personal relationships of life are good, but beyond and beneath them all there is a knowing and being known, a loving and being loved, which to lose is final loss. We accept willingly the claims which life brings, but we also stand willingly under a law that goes far beyond all that human law and custom demand of us.

He presses upon us claims by which our moral capacity is carried past its limit. He bids us hunger for goodness and then bids us recognize that no goodness *we* can achieve is ultimate goodness. He finds in all the immediate goods of life intimations and symbols of an ultimate good. Likewise all the immediate evils of life point to deeper evils. There is a sickness in us deeper than that of a withered hand or a running sore. He points us to an object of devotion in whose service, He declares, we can find inner wholeness and simplicity, be undivided within ourself and from one another.

We are seeking to apprehend the interpretation of the human situation presented by Him whom we are summoned to recognize as the Saving Person. For Him salvation means participation in the ultimate goods, the ultimate joy, the ultimate community, the

ultimate relationships; and deliverance from the ultimate evils, ultimate sickness or brokenness, ultimate
alienation or aloneness or rejection, ultimate death.

Quite deliberately there has been avoided thus far
any use of words wholly central for our theme. They
can be spoken too easily and they are so perplexing.
But they cannot be avoided; "God," "the Kingdom
of God."

The images or meanings which these words call
out occupy securely the overruling place in the picture of life within which the Saving Person finds the
meaning of His own life and the meaning of the lives
around Him.

When He points men to the ultimate standing at
the boundary of human existence He speaks constantly of God. God is the One before whom men are
bidden to be silent, but this One speaks of Him with
entire simplicity and without any anxious argumenta-
tion. He speaks of God as known to those to whom
He speaks. Else what good in speaking of Him? And
yet He speaks of God as needing to be known. Else
why speak of Him?

He does not bid men search for God as a lost object
in some hidden cranny of the universe. He does not
summon men to turn their backs on all the given
immediacies of common life and by some extraordi-

nary disciplines of detachment and of concentration find God. For Him the truth of God is not another truth added to all the other incontrovertible truths of life. For Him God is *the Truth of Life* by whom all the other truths are illumined. God is the true light. Light and the things seen in the light are not found separately and then joined. We only see light when it is reflected on things on which it shines. And we cannot see things apart from the light, whether it be good light or bad light, a rosy light or a bilious light. So God cannot be found apart from life, off by Himself. To find Him we must find ourselves and our neighbors, and look deeply into life and the claims which life brings, into moral failure and death. This One who speaks to us so confidently of God is not claiming to bring us secret information from a distant being. He is unveiling the truth about life, about what is at its heart, its deeper laws, the deeper resources of power, the companionship at its center. The fragments of insight which come to us as His teaching are all fragments of one insight, broken lights of one light. To choose at random—that we live most truly when we love most; that our lives are very precious; that to waste our gifts, many or few, is to waste talents for which we shall give an account; that the maintenance of our inner integrity is a thing worth dying for; that we are brethern in the ultimate relationship; that our choices make an everlasting difference. God is the truth who underlies all these truths, the Being in whom they are all grounded and joined, the living Spirit who gives to life its underlying character.

To share the picture of life which this Saving Person presents to us and within which His own life takes its shape and direction is to acknowledge that wherever a man stands in the midst of life he stands in the presence of Another who is his God. To acknowledge Another to be God is to recognize freely that there is One who is absolutely first and before whom man and everything else are absolutely second. That is hard for man to acknowledge for all men and all communities of men like to think that they are the center, that all things exist for them and are good or bad if they are good or bad for them. To accept God as God is to acknowledge that there is a Holy One for whom I—every I—and we—every we—exist. He is our Maker. From Him and for Him are sun and moon, stars and light, the things that creep and the strange creature, man, that desires and struggles and labors and plans and dreams and must decide. It is not that God was once the starting point. He is always the first and He is always in the center of this picture of life.

To accept this picture of life puts man in his place.

His status in life is that of the servant of Another who is his Lord. The claims that life brings are first of all the claims of this Other. And every other claim, of father or mother or wife or king or community, is only to be acknowledged when it does honor to this Lord. From Him come the voices that speak of things ultimate. It is He who asks not for burnt offerings but for the praise of a just and merciful life. To acknowledge Him is to accept as the first law of life, "I am the Lord thy God; thou shalt have none other gods but me." Whenever anyone else or anything else gets into the first place for man he has turned from the light and wandered off into darkness. If anything gets into the first place that does not belong there, it will be broken. This is all saving truth, ultimate truth, but saving truth can become condemning truth.

Above the confused and struggling wills of men, seeking to shape things according to their shifting purposes, there is Another Will; not a static decree, but an overruling purpose shaping and reshaping the stuff of nature and the choices of men. The business of men is to find their wills within this Other Will. Beyond the partial knowing of men there is Another Knower. The truth of things is their meaning for Him. Men only know themselves and their fellows and the meaning of the events of life truly when this

Other shares with them what they mean for Him. There is nothing hid from His knowing; nothing happens without His knowing, not even a sparrow's fall. Beyond all the caring of men there is Another Carer. There is a likeness to His caring in a father giving good gifts to his children or welcoming home a long-lost son. The true value of things is their value for Him. The price He puts on things and on men is their true price. The business of men is to prize what He prizes. The ultimate claim which comes to men from this Carer is a commandment of love. But love is something which cannot be answered to as commandment. It is not in the power of the human will. It must be given.

This Other is the holy One. That word "holy," so unfamiliar in the vocabulary of our world, speaks of mystery and of depth, not the mystery of sheer darkness or meaninglessness, but the mystery of meaning so full and rich that we know our poverty of understanding; the mystery of light so bright that it draws us but with shielded eyes. It speaks of cleanness before which men know their soiledness, of majesty before which men know their littleness. This Other is the holy One before whom men bow, and only when they have bowed can they stand erect with any safety. And this Other is the abiding One. All else is given over to passingness, to change and decay. Man has his time and dies. The kingdoms of men have their times even though they be long. This One is from everlasting to everlasting. Only that can be everlasting which is taken up and treasured in His eternal life.

To men deeply involved in all the immediacies of life, yet always pressing out toward a limit, this Saving Person comes pointing to the Other, God. Here is the answer to man's ultimate questions and needs. Man can live in full vigor and attain to his full stature only as there is communicated to him his meaning for God and God's meaning for him, only as he is fed by *the word of God*. The ultimate family is the family of which God is the Father. The ultimate community is the community of which God is the King. The ultimate laws are His. His is the ultimate majesty. The ultimate joy is in servitude to Him. In Him are wholeness and peace.

Next to the image of God the image of the "kingdom" dominates the picture of life which we need to recover with as much simplicity and freedom as we can achieve. The kingdom is the realm of existence in which God is fully revealed as God, as absolutely first and all-controlling. It is the order in which the truth of things as they are for God is fully manifested. In the kingdom His will is done, all He prizes is forever treasured and nothing which He rejects is present.

Sometimes the kingdom is pictured as overarching the moving scene of man's history in time as the heavens overarch the earth. It *is* in heaven. More characteristically it is pictured as moving toward men as they move forward in time. It is "coming." As man, involved in all the passing immediacies of life, presses toward a limit, this ultimate order presses in upon him inexorably with ultimate claims and ultimate promise. It stands at the end, as the goal line toward which man is called to strive. It approaches every man everywhere and every community of men, every family in its little history, every nation in its longer history, as a kind of "dead line." Then what has been done has been done; there is no more time to improve on it. It must be presented for what it is. The confrontation between what a man or men together make of the immediate stuff of their little times and the order of God brings judgment. It brings a terrible winnowing, as of wheat from chaff. It could bring applause and sounds of rejoicing for those who least expect them. With the mysterious gift of life there comes an ultimate invitation. So the Saving Person summons men to live expectantly as those who watch.

For Him salvation, the ultimate good, the ultimate fulfillment, is to enter the kingdom, to inherit the kingdom, to be a child of the kingdom, and the ultimate loss is to be shut out of the kingdom, to have no part in it.

We have observed that salvation through Christ presents a kind of middle way between the ways of salvation which would give to some bundle of this-world goods the ultimate place and the ways which bid men turn their backs on the immediacies of life to seek an ultimate quite separate from them. The kingdom to which the Saving Person points men is "above" and "beyond" all the goods and evils of this world's immediacies and men are bidden to seek it first, make it their ultimate asking which is their prayer. They are bidden to put its claims above the claims of houses and lands and father and mother and husband and wife and children. But there is such a thing as having "treasure in heaven" even in the here and now. To reach out to the kingdom is to reach out to it by acts of faith, by acts of love, by acts of forgiveness, by offerings of the self in the service of the King's justice and His reconciling will. Such acts are an investment in it, a partial participation in it. And every partial and passing good of this life truly offered in the service of the kingdom is given back with deepened meaning and worth. The stuff of the king-dom is none other than the stuff of this-world's life raised to a higher power. There is a kind of two-way traffic between the immediacies of this world and the kingdom beyond; man reaching out toward and lifting up the substance of his life into the kingdom; man opening his life in the here and now, his eating and drinking, his working, his relationships, his thinking, his deciding to the penetration of the life and power of the kingdom. "Thy kingdom come, thy will be done on earth."

There is a parallel here with the familiar command-ments in which the Saving Person gathers up the claims under which man ultimately stands. First, thou shalt love that Other, the Holy One who inhabiteth eternity, God. Thou shalt love Him with the energies of thy hunger and of all thy desiring, with thy will-to-live, with thy capacity to work, with thy respon-siveness to beauty, with thy powers of mind, with thy sense of duty, with thy joy in good companionship, with thy struggling will. Again He points us first above and beyond. But the One toward whom he would direct our gathered affections and wills is no self-engrossed deity pleased with the maximum of attention. The God who calls men into His service is Himself faced toward the world and deeply involved in all its immediacies. The human will that is given to Him is carried back straightway by His will into the service of His world. Therefore the second commandment follows directly from the first, "Thou shalt love thy neighbor as thyself." Love for the ultimate Carer and obedience to the ultimate Will involves us again in all the immediacies of life. The children of the kingdom are committed to the service of their neighbor's needs at all the levels and in all the areas of man's this-world life; maintaining life, feeding, clothing, healing; ministering to man's need for truth, education, play, joy, beauty, order, protection from the aggressive egotism of his fellows, just laws, good government, freedom and community. And even in the midst of this service of man on the level of this-world immediacies the children of the kingdom know that the deepest needs of their fellows are centered in their apartness from God, their walking in darkness, their loss of true joys and heavenly treasures, their self-enclosedness.

As we penetrate into the interpretation of life given by the Saving Person we are reminded at every turn that for Him the ultimates and the immediacies of life are bound together. He points us steadily beyond all the goods and evils of our everyday this-world life and yet finds the Beyond penetrating deeply into the stuff of common life. The kingdom penetrates the world of time which we call human history. Wherever it penetrates it brings healing, the restoration of wholeness, the reconciliation of broken relationships, joy and peace. But every actualization of the kingdom in this world is precarious and partial. We are not offered here an earthly paradise. For in this world we are constantly putting ourselves and the things of this world into the central place that belongs to God. Men act as if they were eternal or their earthly kingdoms were eternal, in defiance of death. So the children of the kingdom must live in the here and now in the strength of the foretastes granted to them of a kingdom to come. To them is given the word—"fear not, little flock; for it is your Father's good pleasure to give you the kingdom."

We have been seeking to remind ourselves of the picture of the human situation brought to us by the Saving Person. We must now turn to the life itself, to the way in which His life is shaped and directed by the light in which He sees things, to what He does with His little time and to the total meaning of His life for us men and for our salvation.

What do we see when we look again into the records of this life that have been treasured for us? They are neither still photographs nor movie films such as a "March of Time" recording might provide, shadows of events preserved by an impersonal medium. They are portraits, works of art. Or better, they are dramatic renderings, presenting the meaning of this life as apprehended by those who have been laid hold of by His meaning. An atmosphere of mystery pervades them, of Holy mystery. The matter of fact in them is all seen in depth. Always there is the suggestion that there is more here than meets the eye.

What do we see when we look into these records? We see a man like ourselves, yet how unlike us. He hungers and thirsts. He is weary and sleeps. His earthly life is set in a little sector of this-world time and bounded by a little circle of the world's space. He is profoundly conditioned by the "where" and the "when" of His life. He cannot penetrate with assurance into the immediate future. He must live a day at a time. He is tempted to offer to men as the ultimate a kingdom of material abundance, guaranteeing bread and all that bread represents. He is tempted to set Himself up as the sovereign of an earthly kingdom and to foster the illusion that this is the everlasting kingdom. He is tempted to offer men a kingdom of miraculous powers bringing assured release from all the hazards of this-world existence.

But He takes none of these ways. His whole life makes much of God. He is the willing servant of Another whom he calls The Father. His human will is bent, not without struggle, into conformity with that Other Will. He knows Himself and His fellows held very dear by this Other. He has a sure sense of belonging to this Other, and of belonging to men in relation to this Other. He knows within Himself a joy which He calls blessedness, the joy of a single purpose binding all the broken strivings of life into wholeness, the joy of healing broken relationships. To borrow a helpful phrase from Richard Niebuhr, His life moves steadily "with men towards God,"[1] not seeking solitary ecstasy or release, but taking all the wants and needs and hurts and failures of men up into the light and love of God. And His life moves steadily "with God towards men,"[2] reaching out to men as they are and where they are with the truth of God, the claims of God, the love of God. He sees things from man's standpoint. But at the same time He sees things from God's standpoint. His life is overruled by the vision of a kingdom of which He speaks as one would speak of a known and well-loved city which to

[1] H. Richard Niebuhr, *Christ and Culture* (New York: Harper & Brothers, 1951), p. 28.
[2] *Ibid.*

enter would be very good. It is the homing place for all man's striving. In Him the immediacies of life and the ultimates of life confront one another and are joined. Heaven and earth meet. Things eternal enter into time.

The life which witnesses portray to us is shaped by this apprehension of the truth of things. Here is one who knows what to do with His time. He knows Himself "sent." His mission issues directly out of His double vision; His open-eyed vision of man's need and lostness, clinging to immediacies which can never ultimately satisfy and which pass away, breaking themselves and one another by seeking to make too much of themselves, deaf to the ultimate claims of life; and His vision of God and of the ultimate kingdom. His life is given its direction and drive by being taken up into the circuit of this pull from the tragedy of human need and this thrust from the purpose of God. Therefore He must go to men to teach them the truth of God, His law, His Will, His kingdom; prepare them for their inescapable confrontation by the kingdom; shepherd them; lead them into it; restore them to wholeness by renewing their relationship with the One who is the very ground of their being.

In His own life and person He actualizes the ultimate issues for men. To turn to Him in trustful self-committment, to follow Him, to go His way is to turn to God and the kingdom. To turn away from Him, to reject Him, is to reject God and the ultimate invitation which life presents. His role in the whole drama of human history is to establish the eternal kingdom in the midst of time. He is the Messiah, the Christ. But—and here the mystery deepens—He must establish the kingdom by a cross. He must accept pain and rejection and death; let go all the dear immediacies of life and willingly offer up His life in the service of that Other Will in whom He puts His final trust. To find His peace he must make the world's ills His own. This is a scandal from which those nearest to Him turn away. Shall He who bears the authority of ultimate majesty be dishonored? Shall He who loves God and is loved of God be forsaken by God?

The drama moves forward to its climax. The scandal is fulfilled. But this is not the end. There is a time of darkness and silence as though all the lights on the stage of history were put out for a space. Then to expectant and responsive watchers compelling intimations are given that the defeat on earth, in the midst of life's immediacies, was a victory with God, an ultimate victory. From across the limits of man's this-world seeing, meaning and assurance and power break in. The voice silenced speaks again as a living voice. The presence taken away returns as an unseen presence. Like distant sounds of rejoicing and triumph the assurance floods in that a coronation has taken place "over there" in the realm of the ultimate.

When we come to the end of the story of the Saving Person it is plain, if it was not plain before, that for those who give us the record the most important and potent affirmations about this Person have to do with His ultimate meaning and place in the scheme of things. They have to do with what He is and what He does for God, for God in His relation to men and for us men in our relation with God. They have to do with an everlasting kingdom. They have to do with what lies beyond the limits of the immediate. All the power of what He is and does on earth issues from just this fact.

This does not mean that nothing happens on earth at His first coming, or at whatever instant He comes to men in the midst of their life and time. Much happens of immediate significance, but it is always what has been called "an anticipated attainment," a foreshadowing. At His first coming He feeds some with bread and wine and fish and releases motives in the world which lead to much meeting of men's elemental hunger "in His name." But this feeding is most significant as pointing to another level of feeding and of hunger, to an ultimate sustenance. He heals some who are sick and is the source of impulses that care for the ill and ease pain. But the healings are most significant as pointing to a deeper healing and to a deeper disease, of which a poet can say that "to be restored, our sickness must grow worse."[3] The records say that He calls some back from the very edge of bodily death, though there is no suggestion that those called back do not later pass over that limit. These happenings foreshadow an ultimate renewal of life. He brings into being a new community amid all the communities of mankind, and it shows extraordinary tenacity in history. But the distinguishing mark of this community which gathers around Him as its center is that it carries within itself a light from beyond and possesses an antidote to the forces of decay that destroy human communities from within. He speaks words of immediate forgiveness to those burdened with guilt, but the power of this speaking lies just in the fact that it speaks of ultimate forgiveness by the One who is ultimately offended.

The king comes and is broken in His coming. He is rejected by the many, accepted falteringly by the few. Yet wherever He is received and answered to there are healings, renewals of life, reconciliations,

[3] "Four Quartets," from *The Complete Poems and Plays of T. S. Eliot* (New York: Harcourt, Brace and Company, 1952), p. 127.

new-found community, strange joy. With Him the
kingdom comes. It, too, comes brokenly, marred by
the same powers of this world that mocked the king.
It comes as seed sown, not as full harvest; as a dawning that promises a day. Yet it comes. And wherever
the kingdom penetrates this world the immediacies
of life are transformed. Sanctity enters into marriage.
Children are seen not solely as biological offspring or
inheritors of our prejudices or our social position or
our virtues or our possessions, but as "heirs of God
and joint heirs with Christ." Man's work becomes in
part a vocation. The struggles of man's economic life,
where self-interest so largely rules, are softened and
given a greater measure of mutuality. Even the difficult relationships of politics and government, where
wise compromise is the highest art, are brought under
some ultimate reference that moderates the pressures
from what the contending groups and nations see as
their immediate goods. The pride of men in their
superior virtue is humbled. Death is seen in a new light
that takes away its ultimate sting, but not its immediate hurt. To the extent of these this-world fruits
of the penetration of the kingdom we can set no
limits. Yet they are all partial and incomplete and
draw their deepest meaning from a promised fulfillment which lies beyond the immediate. The given

realities of nature and the baffling union in man of littleness with greatness remain. All the technical problems of life and the limitations of human knowledge go on, even while men's knowledge and mastery of their world ever advance to new levels, tempting men to believe that they are soon to be the lords of creation. The children of the kingdom are always a pilgrim people like the old people of God before them, pressing on toward that light which has dawned.

There are many ways of interpreting for ourselves and for others how it is that salvation is offered to men in Christ. They all have to do with how it is that He brings to men the ultimate goods and delivers them from the ultimate evils. They all center in the relation between men and God, who is the ultimate.

In the following chapters we shall be dealing with two ways of interpreting Christ's saving work. They are not separate ways. They are approaches to two deeply interrelated aspects of one mystery. They find the ultimate evils which confront men in sin and death. Matching these as the ultimate goods are reconciliation and eternal life. We shall be dealing with Christ the Reconciler and with Christ the Bringer of of eternal life.

the Ultimate Evil   3
as Alienation from God

Our business is to help men come
to terms with the issues of ultimate loss and ultimate
gain as these issues penetrate the absorbing immediacies of life—a presumptuous calling, indeed. Actually
our calling is to declare to men and to make available
to men, if only we can, the salvation offered to them
in Christ. But how shall we declare it? It is not sur-
prising that courage often fails us as we struggle for
the understanding of what salvation means and for
the words that will communicate the meaning. We
fall back upon familiar words and sayings in our inheritance. They have the ring of assurance in them.
We repeat them in the presence of the dead and the
dying, in the presence of the sick, of the guilty and

of the perplexed whom we know and whom we do not know, in the presence of the bored and the unheeding. But often we are not sure that we know what our own words mean and we are very unsure of what they mean to others.

And there is the deeper difficulty, always with us: Do we possess in ourselves what we would share? To which the ambiguous comment comes to us out of our tradition: "You cannot give what you do not possess; yet what you bring is not yours. Even a liar may bring men truth. A man may point the way who has not walked it." But our calling will not release us from the struggle. From that calling we must regain our failing courage to assail again the heights of this mystery.

There is put into our hands the story of the Saving Person and with it a bewildering mass of witness and of commentary, to which we are summoned to add our own. What has this Person done for us men and for our salvation? What has happened that is declared to be so decisive for the ultimate issues which men confront? We try to listen again to what this Person says to us. He speaks of ultimate goods and ultimate evils, of ultimate joy, of ultimate relationships, of ultimate death. He speaks constantly of "God" and of the "Kingdom." We cannot hear Him unless these words speak to us. We try to look with open eyes at the Person portrayed in the dramatic renderings of His life and action which have been treasured for us. And we see One driven with quiet urgency to fulfill a decisive role that reaches its climax in a Cross and a Victory. The Cross is clearly planted in our earth amid all its immediacies. The Victory is beyond, "in Heaven," with God, but powerfully witnessed to on earth. At the beginning and at the end "voices" and "appearances" out of "heaven" testify to the meaning of what is seen with fleshly eyes and heard with fleshly ears.

What has this Person done for us men and for our salvation? Or what has been done through Him? What is it that happened in our world or to our world through Christ?

We must be honest in recognizing how many things He did not do which men might want Him to do, which indeed some did want Him to do in the days of His earthly appearing, and were disappointed. He did not solve the problem of supplying men with the elemental necessities of decent earthly existence. The race between the production and distribution of food and the increase of population goes on. Here technology is our hope, not Christ. Disease is still with us. We win great victories not to be minimized, but this enemy reveals a mysterious inventiveness which keeps the doctors and the researchers well occupied. If sheer bodily pain be our problem must we not say that modern anesthesia and drugs have done more than Christ to suppress this evil? The dark fact of bodily death remains. This "last enemy" has been as busy since this Healer came as it was before. If to defer it for a decade or two in the life of the average human in peace times be a great achievement, we must credit that achievement to science, not to Christ. Surely it is evident that Christians have not gained exemption from what have been called "the evils of fortune," from poverty, sickness, imprisonment, this-world sorrow.

Christ has been called a King. There were those who looked to Him in His earthly time to be just that in the primary political sense. But from that high and difficult task He turned away. After His departing His disciples had still to live under unjust rulers; certainly under imperfectly just or competent rulers. He did not solve our political problem, how to give power to rule and yet guard against the abuse of power, how to provide security and order without sacrifice of freedom, how to give freedom without producing chaos or permitting injustice.

In whatever direction we look we must conclude

that His coming has left men struggling with the immediacies of life.

We can look upon the life and action of this Saving Person as we look upon other persons and happenings in the vast current of events we call history. To do so is to exercise our unique human capacity to stand apart in a measure from the very current in which our own lives are caught up. It is to be "objective." It is to place this Person in the moving stream of time and try to estimate how later events were modified or even caused by the fact that He went before. That is to look back upon Him as we look back upon Napoleon or Plato or Karl Marx or the industrial revolution or the Reformation or the invention of the telephone, and to ask ourselves how each of them influenced the course of events afterward.

There is a fact which we can name the Jesus of history. Few deny the fact, though the learned debate as to just what He said or did. Few would deny that this life was among the more notable events of history, judged simply by the aftereffects. But when we seek to trace and weigh the aftereffects or the influence on history, we find ourselves in a morass of relativities. How decisive was this event as compared with other events? What this Jesus of history accomplished was not like the invention of a machine or the discovery of a new medical procedure which changes decisively the relation of men to nature in one aspect, or that whole series of ongoing discoveries or invention which make up the industrial revolution and increasingly alter man's way of life everywhere. It is not like the emergence of a new form of political organization which contests with other forms for the ordering of human communities.

Plainly we must say that a large part of human historical existence for many centuries was not influenced in the least by the appearance of Jesus. As far as human life in China or India or Africa or the Americas was concerned, Jesus might as well not have been born for the larger part of their history. As detached chroniclers of the past we can say that the movement stemming from Jesus has been a major factor in European and American culture, has penetrated as a minority factor into Asia and Africa, and has shown extraordinary survival power. We can credit this movement with vast beneficent results in the realm of human character and human relationships, mixed with much that is tawdry and sordid and tragic. But that this movement has securely *saved* human society from devasting evils in human relationships, or shows any prospect of saving it in that sense, could hardly be concluded from a detached survey of history.

All of which suggests that we are following the wrong clue. We shall not lay hold of the meaning of the saving work of this Person by noting detachedly the impact on history of a figure in the far-off past. Even the contemplation of a believing Marxist could teach us something here. Such a believer does not turn back again and again to Karl Marx because he observes detachedly that Marx has been a powerful force on post-Marxian history. The truth is the other way around. Karl Marx has been a powerful force in history because he was a great believer and kindler of other believers. He was possessed by what he took to be truth, an interpretation of man's total situation and destiny. He won disciples and still wins them. These disciples do not look back detachedly on Karl Marx. They are committed men and it is just they who transmit the influence of Marx on history. The truly powerful figures in history are those whose minds and actions embody and convey an illumination that keeps shedding its light on successive generations. In them something timeless—or long-lived, at least— breaks into time. Only the illuminated, only the disciples, only those who are committed can interpret the secret of their power. Only the lovers of Lincoln can interpret Lincoln and keep his influence alive, not the detached examiners of the record, useful as they are. So this much must be said, in minimal terms, to guide us in our search for the secret of the Saving Person; only those to whom He has spoken and to whom He speaks in the living present can talk with understanding of what He has done for us men and for our salvation.

Does such a conclusion echo for us strange words about a Spirit that bears witness and a truth that can only be known "in the Spirit"?

We turn then to those who testify that He has spoken to them and that they speak in the Spirit. They speak much of a Reconciler and of reconciliation.

We are committed men, with all the hazards of commitment. We believe, God helping our unbelief. Our task is to gain a fresh hold on our belief at its center. Let us then turn away from the role of detached observers, even though we must keep turning to it for the purging of our faith. Let us take our stand squarely within the ongoing community of faith and worship which finds its center in this Saving Person.

Into what a different world of thought we move. Here Scriptures and creeds, prayers and hymns, speak to us constantly of a Saviour and of a great salvation that has been wrought by Him. Writings which are held among us to be foundational and normative and in which we are bidden to hear a Word out of the depths of Being speak to us of One who came into the world to save sinners, to save that which was lost. Voices that are now recognized as coming to us out of our own past testify to us. "God was in Christ reconciling the world unto Himself." "We joy in God through our Lord Jesus Christ, by whom we have now received the atonement." "He is our peace and has broken down the middle wall of partition between us." "God so loved the world that He gave." "My peace I give unto you." "We have an advocate with the Father."

This worshiping community, within which we stand, confesses in its most widely acknowledged creed that "for us men and for our salvation He came down from heaven and was made man." And prayers and hymns reiterate the same theme. "All glory be to thee, Almighty God, our heavenly Father, for that thou of thy tender mercy didst give thine only son Jesus Christ for our redemption." "All glory, laud and honour to thee, Redeemer King." "Lo, the good shepherd for the sheep is offered. The slave hath sinned and the Son hath suffered. For man's atone-

ment, while he nothing heedeth, God intercedeth."
"In the cross of Christ I glory."

It is difficult in the face of this luxuriant symbolism
to choose a key word with which to unlock the
meaning. Perhaps arbitrarily we may take first the
word "reconciliation." The word "forgiveness" stands
close to it. But forgiveness has a more limited connota-
tion and we shall come to it rather than start with it.

Through all the testimony to what the Saving Person has done for men there runs a deeply felt interpretation of what is man's ultimate trouble or illness. Man
is seen as a creature separated from his own ultimate
good. He is far from home. There is a barrier between
him and life. He is not at peace. He is at odds with
himself, with his own created nature, with his fellows,
with life itself. He stands under a condemnation and
rejection from which he cannot extricate himself.
This situation of man is rooted in his alienation from
the ultimate Truth of life, in his transgression of the
ultimate Law of life, in his alienation from that Other
of whom the Saving Person speaks so naturally.

When we turn back from this testimony to look
again at the human scene around us and within us, we
find much to which the word "unreconciled" can be
applied. And there are reconciliations, too, partial but
good in their measure. Man deeply involved in the

manifold immediacies of life knows many forms and levels of alienation and brokenness, and of healing. This is plain even when we look upon our world from a quite human and earthbound point of view, without the benefit of any special light from beyond. If it were not so, common experience would not supply the analogies and symbols which can help to interpret the ultimate alienation and the ultimate reconciliation.

Just because men take delight in the satisfactions of bodily existence and find good the companionships of family affection and friendship, and find shape and meaning given to their lives by the accomplishments and successes of work, radical losses or deprivations or defeats in any of these areas can undercut the will to live. Wherever men find their treasure they are vulnerable in a world in which "moth and rust corrupt and thieves break through and steal." The "heart," taken as the center of man's being and of his attachment to life, can be sorely wounded.

So repeatedly we see those who are unreconciled to something which life has brought them. It may be invalidism or the loss of a son or the inevitability of their own death as something near at hand or the defeat of their party or a failure to receive an anticipated promotion or the realization that they have not the ability they dreamed of having. The more they are wrapped up in any of these concerns, the more vulnerable they are. To say of a man that he is unreconciled with such losses or hurts is to say that he cannot accept life wholeheartedly on these terms. He resists this thing. He fights it off. It stops up for him the springs of joy. It blots out the light. He cannot be at peace with it.

Since all men live largely to themselves—too largely —this issue of being unreconciled or reconciled to life in the face of its radical losses and hurts and deprivations comes home to men most vividly in their individual confrontation with death and sorrow and defeat. But no man lives wholly to himself. All men live partly in others with whom they identify themselves. All men identify themselves in some measure with humanity, even though there is that in them which fights against that identification. Just in the measure of that identification man is faced with the issue as to whether he can be reconciled with human existence as including the dark burdens of hurt and loss and death.

Is this the alienation to which the Saving Person brings reconciliation? Is this the brokenness to which He brings healing?

There is another familiar area in which men know the meaning of being unreconciled, the alienation of guilt. As we have recognized, men make claims on one another. They admire and condemn one another's manner of acting and even the make-up of the person from whom the action issues. Men know what it is to stand under claims. They may even condemn themselves and know the strange uneasiness of not being able to accept what they have done or what they are. The occasions and the forms and the intensities of this experience vary endlessly. A child is shut sobbing in his room by an offended parent. Or a son is burdened confusedly by a sense of having failed to fulfill the hopes which he imagines were held for him. An unmarried mother flees to the anonymity of another city to hide her shame. The white man withdraws from the Negro or even hates him, partly because the Negro is a reproach; his presence brings a hidden judgment.

Guilt may be suppressed into the unconscious depths of being or pushed out to the edge of consciousness. It may thrust itself into the very center. Guilt can be pathological, a form of loss of contact with reality, a sickly self-reproach for imagined wrongs or for a failure to fulfill fictitious claims. But pathological guilt is a distortion of something inescapably real, alienation from the claims which life brings and the self-rejection which follows. Despite all his twistings and turnings man finds himself driven to take responsibility for what he is. "How could I have been so stupid as to say the thing that hurt that other person! I meant no ill. Nothing else occurred to me to say. But if I had been another kind of person I would not have said it. The burden of that failure is my burden."

Is this the alienation to which the Saving Person brings reconciliation?

There is still another area in which it is natural to speak of men's being unreconciled. There is the apartness of man from man, of one man from another man, of whole groupings of men from other whole groupings of men. If the much-quoted proposition be true— "real life is meeting"—there is much traffic between men which is not real life. Two people may simply be strangers to each other, or having met they cannot really meet. They do not communicate. They cannot understand each other. They cannot get together. There may simply be distance between them or there may be distrust or even enmity. A disloyalty, a fault, a stupidity, comes between them. Or they are caught up into the enmities of the human groupings which each represents and the individuals cannot break through these invisible barriers. Whatever the cause, the bars are up. The flow of life to life is blocked. One will not or cannot bring that other into his world of real relationships. There is the crowded anonymity of great cities where men press against one another without meeting. There are the meetings—so called —of the representatives of nations "at the summit" or at some lower level, where men speak to other audiences than to those present and give the impression of hardly meeting at all.

We live in a world that is full of people unreconciled with one another. They may be individuals living under one roof, members of the same family, working side by side, neighbors. They may be alienated groups, whole peoples and nations, whose deepseated fears and resentments smoulder beneath the surface of their guarded dealings and threaten to burst into the consuming flames of war.

Is it this alienation of man from man which the Saving Person has overcome?

The preacher is tempted to exaggerate in order to sell his wares. But we are called to be spokesmen for the Truth of life and must try to put that temptation behind us. Man as we see him in the midst of life's immediacies suffers from these many forms of alienation. Periodically his love of life is radically broken. Yet for most the will-to-live holds on tenaciously. Suicides remain exceptional, even though many play with the idea at some time. Most men are burdened with some sense of guilt, but most men manage to hold it off or ride it out without being overwhelmed by it. All men experience alienation from their fellows and commonly find the justification for it in the unreasonableness or wrongness of those from whom they are alienated.

At the level of life's immediacies there are healings and reconciling powers constantly at work. Just as in the realm of bodily sickness the healing and self-righting powers of the body normally hold in check the destructive forces of disease, so it is in these other areas of man's threatened existence. For the heaviest blows, time is commonly healing. The vitalities of men reassert themselves. New loves compensate in part for lost loves. The invalid finds some little round of occupation to give tolerable shape to a restricted life. Faults are acknowledged and even repented of. There are makings-up and forgivenesses on the level of natural affection. The need to get together provides enough motivation to overcome many misunderstandings or reconcile conflicts of interest or at the least maintain a precarious coexistence.

All of this goes on wherever men are, quite apart from a penetration into their world of a Saving Person. Otherwise life would not go on or be the good, even though the mixed good, which most men find it most of their days. Faith sees in all this evidence that God sustains His world against all the powers that would break it. Despite the provocation He does not give it over unto destruction. "Thou turnest man to destruction: again thou sayest, come again, ye children of men."

These familiar experiences of man's alienation and the partial reconciliations of ordinary this-world life lead us toward the ultimate alienation and the ultimate reconciliation, but they do not themselves bring us to it. It is only when men are lifted up to see themselves and their fellows and their world from a radically different angle of vision that they know the depths of their alienation and the heights of the reconciliation they need. We can find an analogy in social experience. What a man means to himself, what he finds himself to be, is intimately bound up with what he means and is to others. I can only know myself as a son by looking into the face of my father. I can only know myself as a brother by finding that other life held with me in the embrace of a uniting affection that claims both my life and that other life for its own. To see myself as a son and my brother as my brother requires that I see myself and my brother through the eyes of my father. To that extent it requires that I be taken out of myself. Of course, this oversimplifies.

Self-knowledge of my own meaning does not issue from a single confrontation. The very basic truth as to who and what I am—that I am my father's son and my brother's brother—comes to me from many angles. The light of this truth of my being is refracted from persons all about me, often in distorting ways. But the fact remains that I find my own meaning in and with my meaning to others.

So it is with man's ultimate meaning to himself and the ultimate meaning of his fellows to him. These are found, if they are found, in his meaning for Another who is ultimate, the ultimate Knower, the ultimate Carer, the ultimate Willer, God. There have been chosen ones who have been lifted up and enabled to look in broken moments of vision on themselves and their world in the light of that Other's seeing and caring and willing. The recurrent symbolism of the mount-of-vision is significant here. For the chosen have been caught up into communion with One high and lifted up. And they have returned from their confrontation with the Ultimate to their fellows in the midst of life's immediacies, declaring commandments, judgments, promises coming to men from "the high and lofty One that inhabiteth eternity." These chosen ones have been men at once humbled and exalted, seized with a troubled compulsion. They have brought claims that rise far above the confused claims that men make on one another. They have communicated the judgments of a justice that cuts beneath the self-guarding justice of the world. Above all, they have summoned men to look up, to lift up their hearts, to make their ears attend, to acknowledge this Other for what He truly is, and so to know themselves for what they truly are, His people. His people are called to be righteous as He is righteous, merciful as He is merciful, holy as He is holy, to walk their earthly way in the light of His glory.

When the claims of God break through, man knows another dimension of alienation. When there is granted to man a vision of that One, "high and lifted up," in whose light man sees himself and his fellows as they look to the pure gaze of that Other, then and only then does he cry out, "I am a man of unclean lips, and I dwell in the midst of a people of unclean lips."

The Gospel given to us to proclaim is an answer to this cry. Plainly it has to do with a reconciliation of God and man. In propositional terms this Gospel is only intelligible to minds that have learned to think in terms of God and man in their apartness and in their togetherness. As something felt, something entered into by man in the depths of his personal being, this Gospel can be known only by those who have some

dawning awareness of an ultimate Presence that
searches and claims and judges them. The ultimate
deliverance to which the Gospel witnesses is deliverance from an evil which is identified as the dark
shadow cast by a great light.

The ancient name for this evil is sin. That word has
no meaning apart from God. The word sin makes no
sense if the word God makes no sense. It is the name
for something known only in a contrast-experience,
an experience of uncleanness over against cleanness,
of darkness over against light, of profaneness over
against sanctity, an experience of the distortion and
falsity of man's being over against the truth of his
being as glimpsed in his meaning for the Holy One
before whom he stands.

Sin is that in us which separates us from God. It is
that in us which makes us an alien to the order of
being and of relationships in which God's Lordship is
manifest. It is our not hallowing God's name, not
willing His will. It is our obscuring the glory, con-
tradicting the meaning, profaning the sanctity God
gives to life. Deepest of all it is our coming to life and
dealing with life as though God were not real; our
faithlessness, our godlessness; our self-centered anxieties in the face of the insecurity of the immediacies
of life. It is our putting of ourselves, our families, our

race, our nation, in the place of God. It is our refusal
to accept death and our fanatical striving to give a
fictitious eternity to things that pass away. Because
God is a living purpose of love for men and their
relationships and has made us men for one another, sin
is all that divorces us from our neighbor. It is our
doing to him what we would resent his doing to us.
It is our failure to recognize his worth, to count his
hunger and pain and self-respect as important as our
our own, our dealing with him as less than a brother.
It is our complacent acceptance of privilege, our
callousness to the deprivations and injustices which
burden those about us. It is our lovelessness. It is the
dullness of our blinded sight. Sin is our failure to deal
with ourselves as those created in the image of God, as
temples of His Spirit. It is all that weakens and dis-
sipates and disorders the self that God has honored.

Our deepest sickness is not to be found in our sins,
in the plural; not in the separate acts which run counter
to some tidy rules of right or religious behavior; but
in the total state of mind and heart out of which the
separate acts issue as sick fruit from a sick tree. This is
what we understand when we truly hear the Saving
Person speaking to us of what proceeds out of the
heart of man.

All this taken together is "the sin that dwelleth in

me." It is no private thing. It separates man from God whether man acknowledges it or not. This is the ultimate alienation which must be felt and acknowledged if we are to understand the work of the Reconciler.

the Reconciler 4

The Saving Person whose meaning and work we are seeking to grasp afresh did not come into a world unprepared. He came into a particular community, to a Chosen People, a community of belonging. Because that Chosen People knew what it was to stand before the Holy One, they understood and treasured the prophet's word, "Your iniquities have separated between you and your God, and your sins have hid his face from you." Man can be prepared to receive Him as the Saving Person only by being brought into that community of ultimate awareness, by whatever means.

Taking our stand within that community of awareness we ask yet again, what has Christ done, or what has God done in Him for us men and for our salvation?

As we have seen for those who gave us the record of the Saving Person the most important and potent affirmations about this Person have to do with His ultimate meaning and place in the scheme of things. They have to do with what He is and what He does for God, for God in His relation to men and for us men in our relation with God.

Let us move out from that assertion as we seek to clarify for ourselves the heart of His saving action as the Reconciler. In the record He is pictured as One who knows Himself "sent"; sent to restore men to wholeness by renewing their relationship with that Other who is the very ground of their being, sent by the Father. The record was written by men who were assured that this Person had been sent to them. They had known within themselves and among themselves the meaning of alienation and they knew within themselves and among themselves the meaning of reconciliation. The record has been treasured for us most securely by those who have made this same decision of faith.

How did this Person overcome man's alienation and bring reconciliation? We begin with the most simple and obvious answer. In and through this Person God said something, showed something, revealed something to men. What did God say or reveal and how did that change the relationship? Again to give an almost banal answer, God declared His love for men and called out an answering love in those who heard and believed what was said to them. Thus a love relationship was set up and as that is extended among men the saving work goes on.

But even this process is far from being as simple as it might seem at first glance. It means more than that a rarely benevolent man appeared and spoke to men persuasively of the benevolence of God. There have been other at least highly benevolent men in history and they have not cut history in two. The powerful impact of this lover of men and His special significance was from the first bound up with the recognition of a special relationship between Him and God. This relationship was expressed in the parable ascribed to Jesus Himself in the Gospel, in which God is likened to the lord of a vineyard who, having sent his servants, finally sent his son. It is restated in the last Gospel, "God so loved the world that he gave his only begotten Son," and again in the Epistle to the Hebrews, "God, who at sundry times and in divers manners spake in times past unto the fathers by the prophets, hath in these last days spoken unto us by his Son." It is one thing for Another who seeks to be reconciled with us, to send a messenger assuring us of His concern and good will; it is quite another thing to send His son or to come Himself. Especially is this true if the distance is great and the coming is costly.

All these elements symbolized by special *relationship*, *distance*, and *costingness* heighten the meaning of the coming of this Saving Person in the believer's apprehension of it. Love can be measured only by the sacrifices it accepts and the resistances within the lover and in the persons loved which it overcomes. If the lover is given over to passingness and death the love is time-bound and carries sorrow in its heart.

This One who has come to us belongs on the other side of the chasm which separates earth from heaven, or sinful humanity from God. His native environment and true home are within the holiness and glory and love of God. He who is on the side of God comes to dwell on our side. He comes over to our side in order that we may be on His side. He comes to be with us that we may be with Him. This is a divine act of self-emptying, self-humiliation, marked by an immeasurable descent. This person enters into the movement of time. He can be dated. But He is not shut up in time to become simply a fading memory. He is lifted up out of time with power to speak to men and come to men in any time.

The potential influence of this coming is profoundly

conditioned by these overtones of meaning. It is like one who dwells in a region of perfect health going into a plague center; it is like one who dwells in refinement and cleanness going into the animal crudity of some primitive hinterland.

There are few images more surely guaranteed to stir the imagination of men than that of the rescue expedition fighting its way to those isolated by some overwhelming evil; shut in by a burning forest, clinging to housetops and trees amid flood waters, without food in an Arctic waste, surrounded by enemy forces in a battle. The rescuers must pass through the flames, go deep into the waters, traverse the wastes, confront the enemy, if they are to bring relief. And there are more subtle forms of rescue requiring the conquest of less dramatic barriers. There is the patient love of nurses working for months to call out a human response, if no more than a smile, from a child in a hospital for grieviously handicapped children. Such rescuers must bear with the repellent untidiness of these broken lives and the daily disappointment of no response in order to win even a little victory of love.

Believing imagination has seen in the Saving Person a rescuer coming to men isolated by sin from God, from their fellows as ultimately brothers in God, from themselves as ultimately sons of God. The love of

God which is not simply declared but concretely enacted and embodied in this One is a love that descends and divests itself and exposes itself. This is to say what has often been said, that the work of this Person and who He is seen to be cannot be separated. His doing and His being are part of one whole.

The rescuer must make of his life a bridge reaching from the sources of rescue to those in danger. He must get through to men where they are without letting go the food, the water, the resources of healing they so greatly need. If one is to be a bridge-person between God and man in his lostness he must get through to men without losing his hold on God.

The rescuer, on the plane of man's bodily ills and disasters, must make of his life a bridge, and so must the mediator between persons alienated from one another. We can observe this action at many levels of human relationship, of meeting and not meeting. People who do not speak the same language need an interpreter, one who can speak the languages of both and translate sensitively. People whose minds do not meet, even though they use the same words, call for an interpreter who can enter deeply into the alienated minds, one in whose own mind there is a meeting of these sundered minds. For instance, a negotiator for a labor union sought a new contract with the institution in which he had previously worked as a responsible employee. He respected the institution and liked the people under whom he worked. He wanted to represent his union loyally, but he also wanted to be fair to the institution. So he inevitably had a hard time, because the conflicting interests were a part of his own experience.

From suggestions as simple as these we can gain insight into what faith has found in this bridge-Person between God and man, whom our tradition has called the Mediator. The truth of things is their meaning for the ultimate Knower who is God. The true value of things is their worth for the ultimate Carer. The alienation between man and God is rooted in the fact that men do not look upon themselves and their fellows and their world as God looks upon them and do not care as God cares. "My thoughts are not your thoughts, neither are your ways my ways. As the heavens are higher than the earth, so are my ways higher than your ways, and my thoughts than your thoughts." If there is to be a meeting and a reconciliation between the thoughts of God and the thoughts of men it must be through one in whose heart and mind God and man meet. The good news is that such a One has come. Here in one life the truth and love of God penetrate and indwell and transfigure a human mind without destroying the humanity. This One can speak to men for God and speak to God for men. He knows what it is to stand amid the encircling immediacies of life. He can utter to God the cry of human need, even the cry of man's ultimate despair: "Give us this day our daily bread"; "Father, forgive"; "My God, my God, why has thou forsaken?" Yet He can also utter to men the ultimate command and the ultimate forgiveness: "Come, follow me"; "I say unto you, thou shalt"; "Go, in peace." In holding fast to God Christ does not let go of men. In holding fast to men He does not let go of God. In Him God and man meet and the humanity is both broken and restored in that meeting.

To speak of One who reconciles by being in Himself the meeting point of God and man is to lead on naturally to forgiveness. There is no word more characteristic of this Reconciling Person than the word "forgive." He knows Himself sent to forgive. He can give nothing to those who feel no need of forgiveness. The Ultimate One out of whose sending He comes is the Great Forgiver. To accept this Reconciler is to accept forgiveness and to give it. To be of His company is to enter a community of forgiven and forgiving men. He not only speaks of forgiveness and declares it with assurance, He enacts it. He embodies it. The meaning of forgiveness and the assurance of ultimate forgiveness have been declared to men by the whole drama of His life as nowhere else.

Forgiveness is a deep and difficult happening between two persons or groups of persons. It is an overcoming of an alienation more grievous than not-knowing or not-understanding. It deals with offences, with disloyalties, with trespasses, with injuries, with enmity, wrath, and guilt. Forgiveness, on the side of the forgiver, is a way of dealing with another by whom he has been hurt, dishonored, offended, dealt with unfairly, disloyally. If there is nothing to condemn, nothing to be angry about, nothing to reject, nothing by which one is hurt at the center of one's being, there is nothing to forgive. And forgiveness, on the side of the forgiven, is being dealt with in a certain way by another before whom one stands guilty of having hurt that other, of having been disloyal, of having been selfishly heedless, of having been unloving toward another who has a claim on one's love. Otherwise there is nothing to be forgiven. Only in such a situation can the full character of forgiveness be disclosed.

This Reconciler, who knows Himself sent to bring forgiveness, does not speak as though there were simply a misunderstanding between God and man needing to be cleared up. He speaks quite naturally, almost offensively to our taste, of the wrath of God and the judgment of God. The ultimate Love brings a terrible demand. There is wrath in great love. There is a judgment of final futility and aloneness on the loveless. "There shall be weeping and gnashing of teeth."

The forgiveness of this Reconciler has come to men with such authority as being the forgiveness of God because believing men have recognized that He who loved them was the same One who judged them. Only the bearer of the ultimate demands could offer the ultimate forgiveness. He does not depart from God in drawing near to them. Therefore they can come near to God in drawing near to Him. In His forgiveness the rigor of moral judgment is fused with compassion. Because He judges with the judgment of God, He judges His enemies more severely than they judge Him. But because He loves with the love of God, He is the best friend His enemies have. "Father, forgive them."

Forgiveness starts from the side of the forgiver, from the side of the one who is offended, hurt, not dealt with according to the truth and rightful claims of his own being. It is a movement of love reaching out to that other from whom the offense comes. Of course, forgiveness only comes to completion when there is answer on the side of the offender. But it starts on the side of the forgiver. It is something given, freely offered, not something won or purchased or negotiated. It is a love and outreach to the offender that breaks through the flames of wrath and passes over the distance of rejection. Forgiving love does not simply eliminate wrath and rejection. They are subsumed into it and yet carried within it, adding depth and resonance to the love.

Forgiveness on the side of the forgiver is love seeking that which is lost, lost to love and so to life. It is love reaching out to renew broken contact and restore broken relationship. It is love holding the doors of life open to those against whom doors are closed. It is love standing and knocking at doors closed against it.

The forgiver keeps intact within his own heart the relationship which the offender has broken. He keeps alive within himself the image and the meaning which love finds in the offender who has defaced that image and meaning. The forgiving father keeps sonship intact when his son has wasted his hopes for him. The forgiving friend keeps friendship intact within himself when his friend fails him. The forgiving husband keeps the marriage relationship unbroken within his heart when his wife is disloyal. The cost is heavy. The forgiver must accept the hurt of holding to himself a life by whom he is hurt, dishonored, offended. It is always easier to let go, to disown, to break off. For the love of man the burden is commonly too heavy to be borne. But only by holding fast through the pain to the relationship with the other can it be offered back again to the one who has broken it. If forgiveness is to come to its full fruition the offender must accept back again a relationship he has greatly marred. The Prodigal was called upon to receive again his full sonship and all the tokens of sonship; "Put a ring on his finger and shoes on his feet." The father had kept the sonship intact within his own heart when it was well-nigh dead within his son.

The cost and the hurt of forgiveness are borne first by the forgiver and only afterward by the one forgiven.

When we look into the story of the Saving Person the One who confronts us there and speaks to us there is One who sees men alienated from God. They have gone into a "far country," a long way from home. The kingdom of ultimate relationships with God and men is far from them. They do not know true blessedness.

This One, looking on men at war with the Truth

of life finds Himself driven from within to go out in search of them. This One with such an overwhelming sense of belonging, of belonging to the Father and of belonging to men, reaches out to draw men into His own belonging, His own Sonship, His own brother-hood. He is always going over to the side of men, cross-ing the distance between them and God and between them and their fellows. Wherever any are despised and rejected of men there He is as their advocate. Since publicans and sinners are not respectable, He is a friend of publicans and sinners. Zacchaeus is a covetous man, suspected and disliked in the community. The Recon-ciler chooses to put up at his house. At the end He who is a friend of the outcast and the defeated is Himself cast out and rejected of men. And a great wonder takes place. His enemies thrust Him from them. He returns to their side. He pleads their cause with the Ultimate Judge.

And faith looking upon Him sees there the enact-ment in history of the ultimate forgiveness. God comes to us in our lovelessness and callousness and blindness and shut-in-ness, offering us restored relationship, holy communion, and that renewal of life at the center of our being which comes with restored relationship. This is not something simply offered to us. By the self-identification of God with us, it is projected into our world and becomes an illuminating fact of human history. The Sonship which God holds dear for us is here actualized. In the cross and passion faith sees the hurt and dishonor which we do to the True Son and to the True Brother. That hurt and dishonor He willingly bears so that He may offer us a share in His new humanity. "As many as received him, to them gave he power to become the sons of God." We become the sons of God not by futile effort of our own feeble wills to make ourselves as good as He is, but by accepting the renewed meaning He brings and by permitting that new meaning to possess us and grow in us. The new life to which this One calls us is a life lived under and within the forgiveness He brings into our midst.

This forgiveness is not simply prospective. It is retroactive. The Divine Charity does not simply say that if at some future time we have changed our evil ways and return as righteous, we shall be accepted, letting bygones be bygones. True forgiveness is not forgetting. God is not the great Forgetter. He is more truly the great Rememberer, holding the flow of time within the grasp of His eternal knowing. Even assuming that we could return as righteous, an assumption which is false since righteousness is something only gained in the companionship of the Righteous One, we cannot leave our past behind. We cannot leave behind the past of our individual lives nor the past of our humanity. Truly to accept another is to accept the totality of his ongoing life, not excluding the past. We cannot live freely with ourselves unless we can live with our past. When forgiveness is met by penitence and faith men are able to say, "We had not known what love is had we not passed through this, all this, including the painfully remembered past, together." Only the Ultimate Knower who holds the totality and the secret depths of our lives within the embrace of His knowing can offer us the ultimate forgiveness.

All this is not understood in its full dimensions if it is thought of as applying solely to a transaction between God and individual men in their privacy. It is mankind that is the object of this forgiving, mankind in the interconnectedness of our common life. It is the sin of mankind that is here forgiven. Here the broken strands of our human historical existence are brought together. It was the *world* which crucified the Reconciler. It was not the work of some exceptionally obtuse Roman Governor or some exceptionally wicked priests or an exceptionally perverse people. It was the spirit of the world, in which the strong—those in possession of power and place—meet anything that brings criticism or threat to them and theirs with self-protective fear and hostility. It was the spirit of the world in which the dispossessed multitudes turn on him who does not offer them some easy way out of their deprivations and always invite their leaders to promise more than their leaders can deliver. It was the spirit of the world in which those who have brought righteousness within some manageable rules are scandalized by one who embodies a more reckless goodness.

It was the world that crucified the Reconciler and He was crucified just because He was not *of the world*, just because He was dead to the world and alive to God. He was not adapted to the world. He had no position, no possessions, no place to protect, and did not ask for any. Here was One without a grievance. He could meet resentment without resentment. He understood the temptations and the dark motives of His enemies better than they understood them themselves. He could be vicariously penitent for the sins of those who hurt Him and plead their cause before the Father's throne. Only so could He fulfill His calling to be the Ultimate Revealer and Bearer of the love of God.

In the cross of the Reconciler the world is judged. But in the same event "God commended His love for *us*, in that while we were yet sinners, Christ died for *us.*" There is the charity that suffers long and is kind, that seeks not its own, is not easily provoked. There the love of God embodied in the life of the Chosen Man meets the full impact of our common human blindness and self-seeking without resentment, without cynical despair or pharisaical withdrawal, without piling hatred on hatred. This is something to glory in, before which man can kneel and be at peace. All this is directed to *us* in our togetherness, and can be received only by those who acknowledge our togetherness in sin and our togetherness in the love of God.

The core of the Gospel given to us to declare is that God has not left us and our world to be shut away from Him by our wrongness. The One whose love brings to us the ultimate claims of life, who confronts us with the ultimate judgment, and to whom we have made our world so alien, has come over the distance between us and Him to meet us and identify Himself with us. He has made Himself a party to our human history.

We cannot love our world or the totality we call life, we cannot love our fellows or count our own lives as very precious, unless we can see them all as loveable to God. But how can we make our world or ourselves or our fellows lovable to God? It is God who has made it all lovable—glorious though tragic—

by putting His own love and glory into it in Christ. The entrance of this Saving Person into the drama of human history gives to our world a different look than it could have without Him; He and all who answer to Him and all in whom something of His Spirit dwells. And Christian faith has been bold to say that Christ's entrance into our world changes the look of it to God Himself. The love in Christ, the love kindled by Him—yes, the love in unexpected places interpreted by Him—is the reality which redeems the darkness and cruelty of the whole human tragedy. "God was in Christ, reconciling the world unto Himself."

After a manner of speaking we may say that there are three moments in God's looking upon the world. The first was when "God saw everything that He had made, and behold it was very good." The second was when "God saw that the wickedness of man was great in the earth, and it grieved Him at His heart." The third was when He looked upon One sharing fully in our humanity and there was a voice from heaven, saying, "This is my beloved Son in whom I am well pleased." "Look, Father, look on his anointed face and only look on us as found in him."

As man knows the depths of his alienation only as he confronts the ultimate truth of life and sees himself

and his world in the light of God, so his ultimate reconciliation comes from beyond.

Those to whom the love of God in Christ breaks
through testify by word and action that they have
been reconciled to life. They can live with the hard
things as well as the sweet. "I know how to abound
and how to be abased." They can live with themselves
and with their own guilty past. They can live with
people from whom they had been alienated.

The ultimate reconciliation reaches down into the
partial alienations that men meet in the midst of life's
immediacies. They can share something of the blessedness of the makers of peace. For only they can make
peace who are at peace within themselves, those de-
livered from ultimate anxieties, those freed from the
self-seeking which must always be on top. It is those
who have the secret of ultimate security who can be
humble and simple. How could Christ be so humble?
It was because He had heard the Father saying unto
Him, "Thou art my beloved Son." With that He had
no need to defend Himself or to assert Himself before men.

The good news for us is that we can be sharers
with Him by accepting His self-identification with us,
by receiving from Him "a contrite and humble Spirit."
That does not mean that we are to think ill of our-

selves and find little worth in all the dear and difficult immediacies of life. The central joy releases all lesser and passing joys. That joy is known by those who have received from Christ the Spirit by which we cry, "Abba, Father." And in the meaning and dignity which God's love has given to men our uneasy pride is swallowed up in humble and penitent gratitude.

Not that we have achieved; we see through a glass darkly. But life is full of promise. The ultimate kingdom has broken into our pilgrimage through life's immediacies and we walk as heirs through hope of an everlasting kingdom.

the Bringer of Eternal Life 5

We who are called to so weighty a a work pertaining to the salvation of man cannot avoid, even if we would, a repeated confrontation with the dark reality of death. It has often been observed that we retain a professional hold on mortality even when we have lost our hold on life and the living. However absorbed men are in the immediacies of life, death confronted in imagination or in fact stirs the repressed sense of the ultimate. When men are saying farewell to their dead, they rarely fail to give some part to those of us who speak of things ultimate.

Death is linked with a more pervasive fact of human existence, its passingness. Death and time are wrapped up together.

In our human travels over the face of the earth we

can travel many ways. We can travel the same road
many times. We can return again to the home of our
childhood and perhaps find it not greatly changed. If
we take a wrong turn we may be able to go back and
start again.

It is not so in our journey through time. In our
human journey through the mystery of time we can
go only one way. We are always moving onward from
the "no longer" into the "now" and toward the "not
yet." We cannot travel the same road again. There is
no returning, no going back to where we took a
wrong turn to start again. We must always move forward in time from where we are. The moment, the
"now," however precious, will not tarry. A philosopher of another time has spoken of the "the infinitely
thin, constantly changing strip of light, which constitutes the Present, . . . a strip of light marching between a darkness of the Past, which is no longer anything at all, and a darkness of the Future, which is also
nothing."

That figure of "the infinitely thin . . . strip of light,
which constitutes the Present," falsifies our experience
of time. The Present may have a varying span,
measured by the clock or the calender. It may be "the
present moment" or "this hour" or "today" or "this
age" in which our lives are set. The successive and

overlapping "nows" of our private lives and of our common life are made up of the wholes we find in the succession, the task in which we are now engaged, the illness through which we are passing, a meeting with another person, the span of a significant relationship, the duration of a war. The mind and the spirit of men transcend the running moments. Man is dated and time-bound. But he is also one who dates time and so in a measure is a master of time. When we sit with a friend who shares our time with us we do not find ourselves in the presence of a broken moment of that other life. The presence in which we sit gathers the meaning of the years into that meeting. A meaningful "now" draws the past into itself and reaches out into the ever-emergent future.

The meaningful present has a varying span, but it passes none the less. Sometimes we rejoice because "that is over and done with"; that pain, that un-pleasantness, that failure, that time of trouble. But the fact that in our journey through time we are al-ways dealing with what passes away brings sorrow for what was loved long since and lost.

We try to hold on to what passes, to childhood, to the fresh colors of youth, to earlier relationships, to the old, simpler days. Memory can draw the past into the present so that what is no longer can be part of the now, but only brokenly.

All this is true of our individual lives and of our life in community. No one of us can go back into childhood even though the psychiatrists tell us that we may strive unconsciously to do just that and partially succeed at the cost of losing effective contact with present realities. America cannot go back to the time before World War I. Humanity cannot retreat from the atomic age with all its possibilities of burdens lifted and of devastating evils.

Because we have no choice but to go forward into the unknown future we cannot escape the question: Toward what am I going? Toward what are we moving together? Are we going anywhere? Is there anything at the end that will give meaning and glory and fulfillment to all this journey?

Death is the climax and seal of life's passingness. That all men know. Even childhood cannot be long protected from this knowledge. In adulthood it comes in many forms. It comes with the shocking suddenness of an as yet unpredictable "coronary" in the midst of apparent health. It comes in the crash of speeding cars. It comes with terrible deliberation from malignancy. It comes mercifully in the quiet fading of

tenacious old age. So far as human eyes can see it is
utterly indiscriminate. It comes alike to the just and
the unjust. It is no respecter of age or of recognized
social worth. Youth full of promise is taken. Men and
women greatly loved and needed are taken in the
height of usefulness. Release comes tardily to those
who have fulfilled their earthly role and are weary
with failing strength.

Death cuts across every level of our life. Its meaning is tied inseparably to the meaning life has for us.
The condemned criminal in the death house eats his
meal and knows again his aliveness at that level, even
as he knows he will not eat again. The young soldier
soon to return from leave to combat service seeks the
ecstasy of human intimacy as part of his clinging to
his threatened life. For man the worker death is the
end of working; for man the knower and the seeker
for knowledge, it is the end of earthly knowing. For
man the sufferer, it is the end of pain. For man
responsive to the patterns of color and sound offered
him by nature and by art, it draws the curtain on
beauty. Man the decider someday makes his last decision. Since for most men personal relationships, the
bonds of family and of friendship, are the bearers of
the most precious values that bind them to life, the
most poignant hurt of death is in broken relationships.

To be alive is to be communicative, companionable, capable of entering into other lives at many levels of relationship. To be dead is to be inaccessible, impotent, silent, unanswering.

We acknowledge the universality of death in the abstract. We can even fashion defenses for this "last enemy." Without death there would be no room for birth. The population problem is bad enough as it is. Without death there would be no space for growing lives, no opportunities for the successive generations to take their places and play out their parts in history. Death, which breaks life, also gives it wholeness. The story has a beginning and an end. It is completed, though always incompletely, like every story. Death measures the ultimate in courage and in love. "Greater love hath no man than this, that a man lay down his life for his friends." Death measures the ultimate in hatred and in judgment, too: "He is guilty of death."

We acknowledge the universality of death in the abstract but we live in a society that would rather not utter the word. The dead are taken away as quickly as possible. They are not allowed to show that they are dead. A fictitious mask of life is painted upon them that they may not seem to be what they are. The doctors, in kindness, often play the game with us. Unless hard pressed, they do not tell us we shall die.

The minister is often kept away lest his very presence speak of death. Even those who love and watch join in the flight from reality. And love is often cheated of one of its high, hard privileges, the privilege of going through deep waters together with courage and with faith.

Yet within, we know this subterfuge is all a thing of make-believe. We do not quite deceive ourselves or one another. We succeed only in looking away as much as we can. For we know that death is part of life. Each of us from time to time tries to imagine his own death. And in the death of others about us we see an image of our own.

Just because man, despite his deep involvement in the immediacies of life, is a creature who presses out toward a limit, death has for him a forbidding fascination. Man, the fashioner of total pictures of the scene within which he finds himself; man, the storyteller, seeking for a grasp of the total drama in which he has a part, contemplates this limit of death and tries to look beyond it. It calls in question all the immediacies of life. It confronts him with the ultimate.

The face of death is so disturbing just because it is so expressionless. It confronts man at the limit of his existence with a dark abyss. Man may seek to comfort himself with the reflection that it is all quite natural, that while he is alive he cannot know death and when dead he shall have no awareness of it. But he is not securely comforted. Life has offered him too much of light and meaning and good. It has beckoned him on. It has been full of promise at many levels and in many measures. It has even brought him claims and commandments bidding him take hold of the given stuff of his individual life and of his common life and make something worthy of it; make of it what he dimly senses it was meant to be. Does death declare that all of this ends in nothing? Is man confronted at the limit with a meaningless movement of sightless, mindless, loveless matter? Death carries associations of judgment. When a human life is ended men try to sum it up. Is there an ultimate summing up? And what if there be? Man, having spent a lifetime in seeking to penetrate into tomorrow, cannot wholly repress the questions presented to him by a last tomorrow. He both hopes and dreads that all is not ended.

So it is that death as an ultimate evil and some victory over passingness and death as an ultimate good are well-night universally involved in the meaning of that strange word "salvation." Salvation is a matter of life and death. It is that more primitively and more universally than it is a matter of alienation and reconciliation. It does not lose that more primitive meaning when that other meaning with which we have been wrestling takes the prior or central place.

Earlier we noted briefly two radically contrasting ways of salvation offered to men. There are the ways which reject all the interests and strivings of man's everyday life and call him to seek a good quite outside of them. And there are the ways which give the ultimate place to some good found in man's this-world existence. To these we now return with more specific reference to the seemingly ultimate "No" with which death confronts man's affirmation of the meaning and promise of his life.

Despite passingness and death this world and this life present men with impressive continuities that bridge the passing days and centuries. Time by its nature flows, but it is long. Whether man looks into the past or into the future he cannot reach to the limit of time. When he contemplates death for himself or others he reaches for some partial prolongation or ful-fillment of life beyond that limit in terms of the con-tinuities of this world. All human communities, whether family, tribe, or nation, are in part com-munities of memory. So men take some comfort in the possibilities of memory. They will remember or be remembered. They build memorials—and that is good, for some are worthy of remembrance. They propose

to build for some an *everlasting* memorial, to fashion
a false eternal out of the stuff of life's immediacies.
And the fabricators of tombstones co-operate with
these pretensions. But how short are man's memories
for the most part and how many without any memorial! Or again, man pictures his life and the lives of
others dear to him as carried forward beyond the
limit of death within an ongoing community. His life
will not be as though it had not been. He will live in
his descendants. Perhaps they will bear his name or his
very features and ways. Or the good he did will live
after him, not to mention the evil. His life has been
knit as a strand, conspicuous or inconspicuous, in the
continuing fabric of a people or nation. But when
the imagination presses beyond the generations just
ahead how dilute this immortality becomes. The sands
of time are very deep and very absorbent of individual-
ity. Here, too, men clutch at a false eternal to escape
the meaning of death. Such overcoming of death as
man can find in terms of some indefinite prolongation
of a collective life in which he has shared is surely
not to be seen in the assurance of continuing identifi-
able influence or remembrance. That assurance is open
to very few in terms of decades, let alone of centuries.

If man is to find salvation from death in terms of the
ongoing collective life he must be prepared to write

off the abiding significance of his individual life and locate his treasure and his heart in that collective life. And just in the measure that the time span of his knowledge lengthens and he confronts the realities of human history he will be beset by doubts. For the kingdoms of this world rise and fall. In the longer perspective they, too, have their times and the stories of their partial fulfillments and their tragic defeats come to an end. This must be said quite apart from the scientists' imaginative projections of some cataclysm that will conclude the whole human story.

For the most part man's tenacious hopes and fears have projected themselves past death into some dimly pictured Beyond. These projections, whether found among primitive peoples or in the more primitive levels of popular expectation in contempory society, are surely to be acknowledged as free creations of out-reaching imagination, without other grounding than hopes and fears. They are extensions *beyond the limit* of what man treasures and dreads here in the midst of life's immediacies. They picture *some more of the same* indefinitely extended, inviting or forbidding; some more "happy hunting" or bodily delight or family reunion; some more penalties for guilty deeds by burning or torture without the release of death. These are all part of vain imagining. They provide materials for poets and artists. But they are hardly to be taken seriously as promises of salvation, even though they may create imagery that is taken up into loftier versions of man's wrestling with his ultimate destiny.

These projections by man of his passing this-world life out beyond the limit of death must be acknowledged as vain imaginings. They are as pathetic as the broken mirrors and combs and trinkets one sees on unmarked graves of Negroes in South Carolina. But they reveal the inescapable logic that must guide all man's attempts to pierce the barrier of that last tomorrow.

In the span of our this-world pilgrimage our expectations about every tomorrow are founded on what we find as basic, structural, at least relatively permanent in today. There is no way in which we can make forecasts save by projecting into the unknown future the lines we find running deeply through the known and by anticipating that the realities which we find structural or controlling will prove structural beyond the reach of our present experience. This is the course we follow in our immediate this-world plottings of the future. In our larger communal affairs we seek for the great trends (population trends, economic indices, cultural drifts): we search for the basic laws and forces (astronomical forces and recurrences); we try to lay hold of the underlying realities. And when we believe that we have found them we move into tomorrow in the confidence that we shall find them still operative.

Equally, though often quite unreflectingly, the same logic underlies the confidences of our private lives. We put a little money in the bank in the faith that it will be there next year and worth as much or even more, or at least not much less. We feel health and vigor within ourselves, and say to ourselves, "We shall be going on this way for some time yet, and can do some of the things we dream of doing." A boy and a girl are possessed by the power of love. They give themselves up to each other in confidence and look ahead to the fulfillment of what is begun in today. A child falls asleep secure in the assurance of being loved and at home and expects to awake loved and at home. A husband turns home from his journey and expects to find his wife waiting and welcoming. The confidences of tomorrow are all rooted in the confidences of today.

And in all of this expectation today possesses a large part of its meaning and promise because it leads out into tomorrow. We cannot separate today and tomorrow, now and hereafter. A today without any tomorrow is a dark today. To stand as one who confronts nothing but "dead ends," leading nowhere; that is despair, even though we meet it with stoic courage. This is true of our individual lives and of our communal life.

It is false to say that what we do with our lives in the here and now is unaffected by what we dare to trust in beyond the circle that surrounds us. Human life free alike from pride and bitterness, full of action and full of repose, knowing deep joy and deep peace, is life filled with the assurance of being possessed of things—above all of personal relationships—that everlastingly matter and are taken up into some forever and forever. If that assurance be false, as William Ernest Hocking once wrote, "it is only the martyrs that have played the fool; only to the saints and sages the world has lied."[1]

But that assurance, reaching from today into a last tomorrow, cannot be founded on what is passing and given over to death. It is only open to those who have laid hold on the eternal or been laid hold of by the eternal. There is no salvation from death if there is no eternal.

It is part of the restlessness of our time that we have so largely lost the sense of the eternal. We are shut up in time. We know much pleasure, but little

[1] William Ernest Hocking, *Human Nature and Its Remaking* (New Haven: Yale University Press, 1928), p. 439.

beatitude. We have plenty of excitement but little peace. We are without fixed stars to guide our course in time, without central commitments by which to overcome the world. We had hoped that time would show its self-sufficiency, that bad times would give way to better times and lead to some best of all times; that the future would quickly justify the present and give it meaning. But our hope falters. We still hope for better times, but we fear worse times, and we know that we and those to whom we minister will not see the best of all times. What then would fill our time with glory, lifting it from hurried pleasure to peaceful beatitude? Is it true, as wise men have declared, that "all time receives its meaning from eternity"? "What does the world say, does the whole world stray in high-powered cars on a by-pass way?"

Our hearts are restless. Just in the measure that we find no promise of eternal life we reach feverishly to grasp and hold what is offered in the passing now. We clutch at false eternals. In the face of the half-acknowledged insecurities of our individual and communal life we crowd our fellows in grasping for what we cannot keep.

Because we are confronted day by day and year by year with that which passes away, we have a secret hunger for eternal life. We ask the question, "What shall I do to inherit eternal life?" That is part of our hunger for God. But we have, too, a secret hunger for a truth which is not the fiction of our own fears and hopes, a truth that is *given*, before which we must bow in obedient acceptance. That is also part of our hunger for God. And these two, the longing for eternal life and the longing not to be self-deceived, struggle together within us.

To that question, "What shall I do to inherit eternal life?" there have been recurrent voices offering an answer. They have said to men: "Death and passingness are indeed the ultimate evils. To escape from them is the ultimate good." They have spoken of God as the One unmoved, unmoving, changeless, above and beyond all passingness, in whom alone men can come to rest. They have bidden men search within the flux of their own consciousness for the changeless patterns of reason and of beauty which abide and recur within the flux. They have sought to comfort men by assuring them that within every man, stripped of all that is relative, conditional, individual, time-bound, passing, there is an essence which is universal and eternal. They have summoned men to interior disciplines by which they might sink down into a deep center of their being, beneath all the passing show of life's immediacies, and know their oneness with the changeless

Being. Some of these voices have even advised men not to love any fellow mortal too much, since that would bind them to the passing and expose them to the hurt of loss.

It has been a comfort to men to be assured that they are immortal, that death itself is an illusion, not to be taken as ultimately serious. But in the form to which we have been referring it is an uneasy comfort. For not only are we greatly immersed in life's immediacies; what we find precious and meaningful in our own lives and in the lives of others, just when we are possessed by love, is no shadowy abstraction. It is a concrete person, individuated as love always individuates. It is a person with a unique life story, inseparable from his unique body, located in space, distinguished by his own unique pilgrimage through time, a center of concrete relationships—somebody's son, somebody's brother, somebody's husband, somebody's friend—a member of interwoven communities of persons. It is the concrete person that death takes away. The love that gives highest meaning and promise to our lives is not directed to some indistinguishable immortal essence.

We turn back again to the story of the Saving Person in whom our faith and our hope of salvation are centered. He is greatly concerned with passingness and death, and with eternal life. In the actuality of His earthly life He could not fail to be. For He entered deeply into the inheritance of the Chosen People, that community of awareness, the promises of whose history were fulfilled in Him. His way of looking at things was shaped through and through by the Book of His People. That Book speaks everywhere of One who is eternal. It speaks of life. It takes death seriously.

There is no need to pile up quotations. "The eternal God is thy refuge and underneath are the everlasting arms." "Before the mountains were brought forth, or over thou hadst formed the earth and the world, even from everlasting to everlasting, thou art God." "They shall perish, but thou shalt endure." "As for man, his days are as grass; as a flower of the field, so he flourisheth." "Dust thou art and unto dust thou shalt return." "I set before thee the way of life, and the way of death."

Like those who speak to men in that Book, He "came down from his thought of God upon the world; he did not rise from the world up to his thought of God."[2] The dominating awareness of that Other who is eternal heightens by contrast the reality of passingness and death.

[2] A. B. Davidson, *The Theology of the Old Testament* (New York: Charles Scribner's Sons, 1936), p. 32.

The ultimate Knower and Carer who holds within Himself man's true meaning is eternal. The Kingdom toward which this Saving Person bids men bend their wills is the eternal Kingdom. He speaks constantly of life: of the narrow way that leadeth unto life, of entering into life, of that in which life consisteth. He is speaking of life in the here and now. But *life* always has for Him overtones of the eternal. The ultimate evil from which He would deliver men is their alienation from God and the kingdom, not their earthly mortality and passingness. But the God with whom He would reconcile them is the eternal God. Death is not for Him the ultimate evil. "Fear not them which kill the body . . . ; but rather fear him which is able to destroy both soul and body in hell." Fear Him by whom to be rejected is ultimate loss. To men anxiously trying to hold on to life, He declares: "You will not live by always guarding your life, not getting hurt, not getting tired, not getting old. Life is given to be spent, used, given up. Death is the final call to yield your troubled hold on your own private destiny and throw yourself on the Father's besetting care."

This Saving Person looks steadily on the flux of time in the light of "the high and lofty One that inhabiteth eternity." But clearly for Him the eternal is not that which negates time. Rather it is that which comprehends time and penetrates time and gives time its wholeness and its true meaning. The eternal Other to whom He gives the trusting name "Father" is not unmoving and unmoved in some far-off stillness untouched by the restless turmoil of history. He is the seeking, acting, living God, restless in His untiring outreach for the lost. He enters time and speaks in time. His kingdom invades history and the kingdoms of this world. Yet He remains Lord of time. For Him the present does not crumble away, as it does for us. History and the embodied spirits who make history find their abiding meaning and reality only as they are gathered in, judged, purged, costingly redeemed in the eternal life of God. Of that gathering of time into wholeness man has a broken intimation in his own partial capacity to hold the passing in a living present, and even to find the hurts and failures of his past taken up and redeemed. The Saving Person makes His own that perplexing symbol, resurrection. Death *is* a shattering end of man's life in time. But it is just that concrete individualized life in time, taking up into itself the stuff of life's immediacies, which is confronted at last by the judgment and the mercy of the eternal Carer, and lifted up to a place of acceptance or of rejection in the order in which the truth of things as they are for God is regnant.

Before such a mystery the mind and imagination of man must be humble and undemanding, content at the most to "see through a glass darkly."

The apprehension of the truth of things communicated by the Saving Person as part of His own self-giving and self-disclosure shaped His life in time. He looked steadily with open eyes on life and death. He rejoiced in the lilies of the field, which today are and tomorrow are cast into the fire. He loved as we have not learned to love. Yet he never clutched anxiously at life. He spent it freely, with urgency but without panic haste. He had only a little time. He was not anxious for the morrow. He made no elaborate plans to perpetuate Himself. Those short unhurried years were so filled with meaning and power that they have overflowed with meaning and power into the lives of men in all the years that have come after.

What was the secret of time so redeemed? The secret was that He walked His brief way in the light of the eternal. He knew well the passingness of life, but amid all the passing He was held fast in the abiding Companionship. To men clutching at things that pass away He said in His own way, "You cannot take it with you." Quite simply He spoke of "treasures in heaven." There are things which cannot be taken away because God lifts them up into His eternal kingdom and treasures them, to be reclaimed at the last by those who can be recognized as their possessors, with surprise—acts of love for God and for men, faithfulness to God and His cause. Because He wholly trusted the love of the Father who claimed Him He trusted the promises of that love. And whenever He saw in the passing days anything which answered to the love of God—an act of true penitence or faith or mercy— He was assured that God had laid hold of this and would have it in his keeping forever. Because He wholly believed that the love of God overrules all the passingness of time, He was confident that at the last God would sift and lift up into His kingdom all that is dear to His love and cast away all that betrays and dishonors it. So it was that the light of the eternal lighted with glory His little passing time.

The whole Gospel is the story of the coming into man's world of a life-giving Life. It is the story of a Life that came from God and went to God. Here the very Truth of God and the very Life of God and the very Love of God are embodied in a truly human life. And the human life is transfigured by the light within it.

At the beginning there were those who answered to Him and grew in the assurance that the life they found in Him was the true life in which they were called to share. He was God's very Presence among them, and in that Presence their lives were lighted up and filled with promise. In Him they had a foretaste of eternal life.

When He began to tell them that He, too, must enter the dark realm of pain and death, they were astonished and cast down. "It cannot be so, Lord, that One who is so dear to the Father should suffer this and die." But He said it was so. And it was so. "He suffered under Pontius Pilate, was crucified, dead and buried."

Terrible doubt possessed those who loved Him and had begun to put their faith in Him. Was He and was the life He had brought them only passing like all the rest?

And then in ways that outran all their powers of telling and baffled their understanding His living presence and power were manifested to them. His strengthening love flowed into them. The meaning of His life broke in upon them as it never had in the days of His bodily presence. They were knit together in His dear companionship. They could almost believe now in that testimony, "He that loseth his life shall find it." They were assured that the life which triumphs over death is His life and that by sharing in His life they could share in His victory.

Out of those years that are past there come to us the testimonies of which we are called to be the bearers in our time. "Because I live, ye shall live also." "This is life eternal, that they know thee the only true God, and Jesus Christ, whom thou has sent." "Who shall separate us from the love of Christ?"

He came in a moment of time, but as T. S. Eliot has put it, "A moment in time but time was made through that moment: for without the meaning there is no time, and that moment of time gave the meaning."[3]

We still walk amidst the passing. We are still given over to death. But we walk as those united in faith with Him who has been lifted up out of the passing away that haunts us, bearing the wounds of our human wrong, and who offers Himself in every present time as the hallowing, reconciling, life-bringing Presence.

Here we remember Him, who is the dearest, holiest part of our human past.

Here we have communion with Him who is the cleansing center of our human present.

Here we look forward to Him who is the crown of our human hopes.

[3] From *Collected Poems 1909-1935* by T. S. Eliot, copyright, 1936, by Harcourt, Brace and Company, Inc. and reprinted with their permission, and that of Faber and Faber Ltd.